GW00975914

One Man's Vision

The Story of the Norfolk and Norwich Association for the Blind, 1805–2005

Frank Meeres

Patron:
Her Most Gracious Majesty Queen Elizabeth II

NNAB

Published by the Norfolk and Norwich Association
for the Blind 2005
Registered Charity No. 207060

© The Norfolk and Norwich Association for the Blind 2005

The Norfolk and Norwich Association for the Blind asserts
the moral right to be identified as the author of this work.

A catalogue record for this book is available
from the British Library.

ISBN 0-9549912-1-4

Printed and bound in Great Britain by
Norwich Colour Print Ltd., Norwich

Design and typesetting by
Spire Origination Limited, Norwich.

All rights reserved. No part of this publication may be
reproduced, stored in a retrieval system, or transmitted, in
any form or by any means, electronic, mechanical,
photocopying, recording or otherwise, without the prior
permission of the publishers.

Contents

THE BISHOP OF NORWICH
BISHOP'S HOUSE
NORWICH NR3 1SB
TEL 01603 629001 FAX 01603 761613
E-MAIL bishop@bishopofnorwich.org

FOREWORD

It was an excellent decision of the trustees of the Norfolk and Norwich Association for the Blind to commemorate the bicentenary of the Association by publishing this History. It was an inspired choice to ask Frank Meeres of the Norfolk Record Office to research and write it.

In 1805 Thomas Tawell founded what now seems the quaintly named *Institution for the benefit of the indigent blind in Norfolk and Norwich*. He was concerned by the plight of both the young and elderly blind in the area. This book traces the history from those early stages through to the present day when the Norfolk and Norwich Association is helping some 16,000 local people. The needs have never been greater.

Throughout the past two centuries the underlying purpose has been to care for those whose sight is poor and are in need of help. This is just as necessary in 2005 as it was 1805. The imaginative ways in which the needs of the blind and the partially sighted are met by this Association continue to impress and inspire me. I am delighted that this well researched history is now available. I hope that it will help many people realize afresh what a great asset this Association continues to be in the life of our city and county.

+ Graham Norvic:

The Rt Revd Graham James
Lord Bishop of Norwich
President, Norwich and Norwich Association for the Blind

Chapter 1

The Beginnings

Norfolk and the history of the treatment of the Blind

The connections between the welfare of the blind and the county of Norfolk go back a very long way. In the *Domesday Book,* compiled in 1086, there is a reference to an unnamed blind man who had three acres of land in Martham. The first known asylum for the blind was built in London by a merchant named William Elsing in 1329: his surname could indicate that he, or his ancestors, came from the village of Elsing in Norfolk. One sixteenth century Bishop of Norwich, Richard Nix, was known as 'the blind bishop'. He was not born blind but became so towards the end of his very long life. He was already about 56 years old when he became Bishop in 1501 and lived to be almost 90. The historian Francis Blomefield describes him at his death as 'having been many years blind and decrepid (sic)'. However, he remained active as a Bishop to the end, acquiring a reputation for the severity with which he dealt with heresy in the diocese. He built the transept vaults of Norwich Cathedral in stone after the major fire there in 1509 and his magnificent tomb can still be seen in the south aisle of the Cathedral nave.

The City of Norwich conducted a census of the poor in the city in 1570. Several blind people are recorded. They include 67 year old Thomas Damet, a cobbler by trade 'that work not for that he see not':

His wife and daughters, including one of only eleven, earned money by spinning wool. Eighty year old Cicely Reves lived alone and was blind and unable to work: she was receiving alms of just two pence a week. More supportive communities could also be found. Richard Sandlyng, 54, was blind and unable to work. His wife, and adult child, spun wool. They had also taken in a 12 year old orphan boy who acted as guide to Richard. Another blind man, William Mordew, although 70 years old was still working as a baker, and owned his own house. His wife was also earning money from spinning.

The 1601 Poor Law Act laid down that the relatives of every poor, old, blind and lame person must care for them. If there were no relatives, then it was the responsibility of the parish in which they lived to undertake the care. This could either involve payments to people living in their own homes, or it could mean looking after them in the parish workhouse.

The first 'modern' home for the blind in Europe was the Institution des Jeunes Aveugles, which was founded in Paris in 1785. Its main aim was to teach its inmates to read and write, but it also gave some training in handicrafts. The first Institution in England opened at Liverpool in 1791: its founders included two blind men, Edward Rushton and John Christie. The Institution aimed to train the blind in making products, especially basketware and sailcloth, and to finance itself from the sales. Similar institutions followed over the next few years including at Bristol in 1793 and at Southwark, London, in 1799. The school in Paris was funded by the National government but the English institutions were different. They received payments on behalf of parish authorities for their inmates, which sprang ultimately from the 1601 Poor Law Act. However, these usually barely covered the costs of maintenance and the Institutions depended heavily on the generosity of local people.

Norwich in 1805

Medieval Norwich was the largest provincial city in Britain and the area enclosed within its city walls was even larger than that within the walls of London. In fact it was so large that there were many areas of land within the walls that were not built on: for example, the house of Lord Bradford, on Magdalen Street, had a garden of almost four acres.

By 1800 Norwich had been overtaken in population by Bristol, Birmingham and Manchester, but it remained a wealthy and flourishing city. The population in 1801 was 36,906, with 12,267 engaged in trade, manufacturing and handcrafts. The real population was probably greater: it was noted that the city had furnished at least 4,000 soldiers and sailors to fight in the war against Napoleon. The city's wealth had been built on weaving. Whilst this had been the making of Norwich in the Middle Ages, there had been a decline in the sixteenth century. As a result the authorities had invited 'strangers' into the city – men and their families from the Low Countries to kick-start the industry. This they did very successfully. They also enriched the city by bringing in their own cultural ideas. Norwich was very much the provincial capital for East Anglia and by 1802 there were five banks in the city. The Norwich General Assurance Company was set up in 1792 and the Norwich Union Fire Office in 1797, both by Thomas Bignold.

Norwich is still known as a city of churches. In the early nineteenth century there were 35 Anglican parish churches within the city walls, as well as the Cathedral church in its Close. There were strong Nonconformist groups too – Congregationalists at the Old Meeting House, Presbyterians at the Octagon, Baptists in St. Mary's and Methodists at the Tabernacle. There was also a large community of the Society of Friends and a Roman Catholic community in the city, the latter with a newly-built chapel in St. John's Alley. All these communities had a strong caring element within them.

As in all communities there were rich and poor, able and less able within the city. It is hard today to think of a society with no state provision for the old, the sick and others who for whatever reason were unable to provide for themselves. The Georgian era was in some ways a cruel and a violent age: it was also one in which many great charitable deeds were done. The consequences of some of these, like the Blind Institution, are still with us today.

Norwich had a reputation as a caring city. A. D. Bayne wrote: 'there is hardly a town or city in the kingdom, of the same population and extent as Norwich, in which a greater amount of charity exists and where institutions for the relief and comfort of the sick and the poor are so abundant'. The Great Hospital, founded by Bishop Walter Suffield in 1249, is the only medieval hospital in England to continue down to the present day. Examples of seventeenth century charitable foundations include the Boys and Girls Hospital founded in 1618 by Thomas Anguish, and Doughty's Hospital, founded by William Doughty for the poor and infirm in 1687.

The Bethel Hospital for the Insane was built by Mary Chapman in 1713 and appears to have looked after some of her own relatives with mental problems. She lived in it until her death in 1724 and it was formally founded under the terms of her will. Mary was born Mary Mann, the daughter of John Mann, a wealthy Norwich merchant: her husband, Samuel Chapman, was rector of Thorpe St. Andrew. She is buried in the chancel of the old Thorpe St. Andrew church: the tombstone is in the open air, as the church building now has no roof. The stone reads: 'she built at her own expence the house in Norwich called Bethel, for the reception, maintenance, and care of poor lunatics, to which and other charitable uses she gave all her incoms while she lived and her estate at her death'.

The idea of a hospital for Norfolk and Norwich was originally proposed by Thomas Hayter, the Bishop of Norwich between 1749 and 1761. The idea lapsed after he left the city but was revived by William Fellowes and Benjamin Gooch. Founded in 1771 as a charity, the hospital only took patients whom subscribers had recommended as being unable to afford to pay for medical treatment. People who were brought into the hospital after accidents were admitted but, if it was later found that they did have money, they had to pay for both their subsistence and their medical care. The hospital was not large: originally it had one hundred beds. There were two dozen private doctors in Norwich, the most well-known were Philip Meadows Martineau and Edward Rigby. Some doctors gave their services free to the poor. James Alderson prescribed free of charge at his house in Colegate every morning: up to 500 people a week might attend. In 1803 the Norwich Public Dispensary was instituted to give advice, medicine and attendance to those who could not afford to pay.

The city's contribution to prison reform is a well-known one. Elizabeth Fry, born Elizabeth Gurney in Magdalen Street, devoted her life to the care of prisoners and to the improvement of their conditions. The Gurneys were a prominent Norwich family, merchants and Quakers: Elizabeth was brought up in the family home at Earlham Hall.

Other Institutions were founded in the years after the foundation of that for the Blind. The Norfolk County Lunatic Asylum was built in 1814, and was only the third of its kind in the country. The Eye Infirmary was founded in 1823 by three men who were also on the staff of the Norfolk and Norwich Hospital, Lewis Evans, Robert Hull and Thomas Martineau. The first premises were on St. Benedict's Plain but moved, in 1854, to a house in Pottergate.

Chapter 2

1805–1854

Thomas Tawell

The Blind Institution has survived and flourished through two centuries thanks to the generous support of many Norfolk individuals and families. Its foundation, however, is entirely to the credit of one man, Thomas Tawell. Tawell was born at Wymondham in 1763. His father, Henry, was a wealthy draper, his mother, Mary, a member of the Colman family. Both families had interests in the Wymondham area and the couple had married in the parish church in 1750. They had two children: Hannah and Thomas.

When Thomas was just ten years old his father died. He left some land in Wymondham to his brother William, £1,000 in trust for Hannah, and the rest of his property in trust for Thomas. One of the trustees was Thomas' uncle, Thomas Colman, a Norwich ironmonger. Henry Tawell had been a man with an enormous range of intellectual interests. He had a large library of books, and collections of coins, fossils, microscopes, telescopes and mathematical instruments. Under the terms of his will, Hannah was to be allowed to choose fifty books: the rest of the collection was to go to Thomas when he was 21. Henry saw Thomas Colman as the natural guardian of his son. Colman was to use rents from Tawell's property for the 'maintenance and education' of the boy. Unsurprisingly, Thomas Tawell himself became an ironmonger.

Bust of the founder, Thomas Tawell

Thomas Tawell never married and in 1804 he was living in the Upper Close in Norwich. It was from here that the Institution was launched. He had been affected with blindness himself, but whether through illness or an accident is not clear. In his speech of 17th January, 1805, he stated:

'There are few present I dare say, Mr Mayor, who are not fully aware of the circumstances under which I have laboured, with regard to my loss of sight; and I hope I shall have credit for it when I say, that none can possibly feel more sensibly than I do, for the miseries of all those whom it hath pleased God should be afflicted in the same unhappy manner.'

Thomas Tawell issued an open letter on 1st December, 1804:

'I have for some time cherished an inclination to attempt, at least, the establishment of an *Institution for the benefit of the Indigent Blind in Norfolk and Norwich*; and I cannot but express an earnest wish, that in case my attempt should be favourably received, an enlargement might be made on the plans which have hitherto been adopted, by uniting with a *School* for the *Young*, an *Hospital* for the *Old*.'

He pointed out that societies for the instruction of the blind already existed in London, Liverpool, Bristol and Edinburgh. Why should Norwich lag behind?

The first public meeting was held at the Guildhall on 17th January, 1805. The mayor of Norwich, James Marsh, was chairman. Tawell spoke at length and he pointed out that none of the already existing societies in other towns were doing anything for the aged blind:

'They hold out for the patronage of the public, an Asylum for the benefit of the Blind: and here comes one who, to the miseries of a total blindness, adds also, that of extreme old age and helplessness: none to whom he belongs can afford him either consolation or assistance, and to this person their answer is, "No, as you are so old that we cannot teach you with a view to your helping yourself; our Charity extends no further, and we can do nothing for you".'

Tawell was clear in his own mind: his proposed Institution would care for the old as well as educate the young. In fact, Tawell had taken decisive action already: he had found the place for the new Institution:

'I thought, Mr Mayor, that I had no right to ask the public, although in behalf of those of so superior claims upon our benevolence, for more than have been ventured upon in any foregoing case, unless I myself gave a corresponding proof of my faith and sincerity in the scheme. I have therefore bought a large substantial house and three acres and a half of ground, situated in Magdalen Street, late the residence of Thomas Havers esquire, and I believe at present inhabited by the Right Honourable Lord Bradford; and I now beg leave to make a tender of my interest in these premises, for laying the foundation of such a Society as I have mentioned, agreeably to an outline and proposals which are already prepared, and which I have now the honour of presenting to this Meeting.'

The next step was to publish the Rules for the Institution:

Laws for the Admission of the Aged

No person to be admitted who has not obtained his or her age of 65 years.
No person to be admitted who has been maintained in any House of Industry, Work House, or Parish House, within the last 12 months.

No person to be admitted who has for the last 12 months constantly received parochial relief.

No person to be admitted who has been a Common Beggar, or Wandering Minstrel, or played on any instrument at Ale-houses.

The Committee to select Objects, and admit them as vacancies arise; and if the claims of two or more Applicants shall be judged by the Committee to be equal, the admission shall be determined by lot.

The Committee to have full power to discharge any person for improper conduct.

Every person, on admission, to bring one complete Suit of Apparel, as shall be deemed sufficient by the Committee – a bed, and one guinea towards funeral expenses.

Laws for the Admission of the Young

No pupil to be admitted under the age of 12 years.

If the party on whose behalf the application is made be chargeable to the parish, it is required that such parish shall contribute a weekly allowance, to be settled by the Committee, towards the maintenance of the pupil.

If the parish be at a distance from Norwich, some respectable housekeeper in the city shall become responsible for the regular payment of the sum stipulated.

It is also expected, that in all cases some respectable person resident in Norwich shall engage to take back the pupil when discharged from the School, either in consequence of being sufficiently instructed, or on account of misconduct, or for any other cause; and likewise to defray the expenses of the Burial, if the pupil die there.

The pupils are to be kept in the School only until they have attained a sufficient knowledge of their trade, and at all events not more than three years.

Laws for the Admission of both Old and Young

No person to be admitted into either the Hospital or School who does not belong to some parish in the city of Norwich or county of Norfolk, or who hath not resided in Norwich or Norfolk for at least seven years.

The Committee would in effect ask for references for each applicant. A medical gentleman was to give a statement as to the nature and cause of the blindness of the applicant. A clergyman had to answer questions about the applicant's residence, previous way of life and family. There was a moral element to this. They were specifically asked to say if the

Early drawing of the Institution

applicant had been a beggar or minstrel within the last two years, and also a more general question: 'Does the person bear a character of regularity, decency, and sobriety?' In cases where poor children were to be admitted to the School, the 'respectable' person in Norwich who would pay the allowance, and take back the child when discharged, had to be named.

The meeting heard that £1,000 would be needed to set up the establishment, with a sum of £700 a year to support it. It unanimously resolved that the Institution be established. A second meeting was held on 25th April. Already a good deal of financial support had come in: almost £740 in immediate cash, together with offers of annual subscriptions of over £336. The Bishop of Norwich was appointed President, Robert Fellowes and Richard Milles vice presidents. Four trustees were also appointed: Jeremiah Ives of Catton, Robert Harvey junior of Norwich, Thomas Kett of Norwich and Thomas Cubitt of Honing. A Committee was appointed which consisted of sixteen people – all men and many of them leaders of Norwich society. They included Tawell himself, John and Joseph Gurney, John and Robert Herring, and Elisha de Hague, the Town Clerk of Norwich. Six members of the Committee were clergymen. Three auditors were appointed.

By the end of 1805 about 250 people had made one-off gifts, or agreed to make annual payments – many did both. They included some people whose names were to be part of the Institution's history for generations, such as Thomas Back. Captain Irby and his wife each gave five guineas in cash and promised two guineas annual subscription. The artist Robert Ladbrooke subscribed a guinea a year. Country gentry also contributed. Lord Wodehouse gave twenty guineas, Thomas Coke MP gave the same and a yearly subscription of two guineas, and this was matched by Thomas Bagge of King's Lynn. Others included five members of the Gurney family, seven members of the Ives family of Catton, Robert Marsham, Francis Noverre, Joseph Peckover, William Smith, Mr Sewell of Catton, and the Dean and the Bishop of Norwich.

These names show that the new Institution was receiving support from all elements of Norwich and Norfolk society. The Church of England was strongly represented but so were other faiths: Peckover and the Gurneys were Quakers and John Basely, the Treasurer of the Institution, worshipped at the Octagon. Smith was on the left in politics – he was always known as 'the radical MP for Norwich' – whereas Coke, Back and Ives were prominent in the local Tory cause.

The early years

The Committee started to meet in May 1805. Generous offers of support were recorded. Mary Mountain offered to act as Matron without a salary, James Mills to shave and cut the hair of the blind for nothing. Edward Colman offered to act as surgeon, and to supply medicines without charge, and Dr Warner Wright offered his medical services.

The Committee decided to advertise for a basket maker able to instruct blind children; he was to be between 25 and 45 years of age and capable of reading, writing and keeping common accounts. A man called William Swan was the first to answer the advertisement. However, the Committee chose another basket maker, Wortley Green instead. He was willing to undertake the work for a pound a week, four shillings less than Swan proposed. Green at once went to Suffolk and Cambridgeshire in search of osiers for the work. He worked for the School for two years, but had his own problems. In August 1807 he was dismissed for drunkenness. His behaviour, which had in any case 'at various times been very exceptionable', was climaxed by a two day absence from work previous to

Assize Week. William Swan received his chance after all, and succeeded Green as the teacher of basket making in the following month.

In September, the Committee were ready to take in pupils. It looked at the cases of three people. First came Robert Watts, who was from Nacton in Suffolk, aged 21 and totally blind. He wanted to be taken in for instruction. His father was willing to pay for his board but the Committee decided to postpone a decision for some weeks, as he did not really fit the criteria they had in mind. Five months later it decided to admit Watts, possibly influenced by the agreement of his father to pay eight shillings a week for support. However, they made it very clear that the case was not to set a precedent and that people like Watts were not to take the places of those for whom the School had been established. The Committee probably regretted their decision to admit him: in July 1807 it found out that Watts had married 'a late servant of this Hospital'. It decided that this amounted to improper conduct and ordered his father to take him away as soon as possible. However, it allowed him to continue as a day scholar.

The two other people whose cases were considered at the first meeting were both 25 years old – Samuel Blaseby of St. Michael at Plea in Norwich and Sarah Wells of Weston. Both had some means of support: Samuel was receiving fifteen pence a week from the Board of Guardians, while Sarah received three shillings a week from her parish.

Sarah and Samuel were both accepted at the beginning of October along with 21 year old Sarah Base or Bace of St. Edmund, Norwich, 12 year old Sampson Fox of Catton and Isabella Wright, 37 years old and from St. Michael at Thorn in Norwich. On Monday 14th October these five were formally admitted to the institution as its first occupants. Others soon followed and it became customary for Guardians of the Poor (in Norwich) or parish Overseers elsewhere to make a payment of two shillings a week for the upkeep of each person from their area admitted to the School.

There were some variations in the general pattern. Thomas Brown was admitted as a day scholar. He was to have his dinner with the pupils and return to his parents in St. John Sepulchre each evening: a walk of some two miles along Magdalen Street and King Street. When Robert Arnold, a 73 year old Chelsea Pensioner, applied in February 1806 he was told that he would have to provide his own clothes out of his pension. He decided against coming in.

By February 1806 twelve pupils had been admitted to the School. They were offered training in three skills – making baskets, spinning flax and braiding sash-line. Most of the pupils were learning two of these skills. Only one pupil, Sarah Bace, had been discharged: sadly she was judged to be 'incapable of receiving instruction'. The first two elderly people were admitted on 22nd January, 1806. They were Frances Kenney, aged 67, of Gressenhall, and Anne Moore, 72, of Wreningham.

In April 1806, the first financial accounts were issued by Basely. The only members of staff receiving salaries were Walter Green, the Instructor, who was being paid 20 shillings a week, and a woman who was employed to teach spinning at a wage of six shillings a week. Interestingly, Green was paid £12 for his expenses in going to Liverpool to see for himself how the Institution there was working. It had been running for 12 years and always saw itself as a role model; 'when the Institution is established and found beneficial the plan when corrected and amended by experience [will] be published to produce imitation in other places'. By 1800, there were 68 pupils in the Liverpool Institution, employed in several workrooms. Almost all of them were supported by parish poor relief. There was a strong religious aspect: inmates had to go to church twice each Sunday and were catechised once a week.

However, Liverpool was having some problems. Experience was showing that blind people who had already been earning a living playing music in streets or inns were a disruptive influence – they were refusing to learn any 'useful industry'. Musical instruction at the Institution deliberately excluded fiddle playing. In fact quite a large number of the early intake at Liverpool had proved incapable of training. Of 22 pupils who passed through in the first five years of operation, only five were found to be attempting work in a trade that they had been taught. Nine others were playing music in the streets and begging. Between 1800 and

1802, 35 people left the Institution, only ten were sufficiently trained to be able to support themselves. The problem was that the Institution was taking in too great an age range, up to 45 years old, or even older in a few cases. These people were less able to adapt to the new skills than were the younger ones. The Institution also cut back on admitting women, for whom they had little to offer: those who were capable of it could undertake music training, but the only other trade was needlework. (By the 1830s, 74% of the pupils at Liverpool were under 20, and over half under 16. Males were outnumbering females by three to one.)[1]

Norwich learned the lesson: it was necessary to be very careful that the people who were admitted could benefit from what was on offer. In August 1806, Robert Loome of Heckingham was refused admission as 'he was not deemed by Dr Wright and Mr Colman to come within the intention of this Institution as he has a Sufficient Portion of Sight left to prevent his relying upon his feeling to receive his instruction in Basket Making etc as a blind person'. It was decided that anyone wanting admission would be first examined by Colman and Wright as to the exact state of their eyesight.

The two men had delicate decisions to make. Applications in 1807 included those from Amelia Storey of Yarmouth, 'totally blind', Mary Brook of Norwich 'nearly Blind and incurable' and Robert Bird of Oulton 'not totally blind'. Wright and Bird examined Bird – who was only 12 years old – 'their opinion was that he possessed too great a degree of sight to be capable of receiving the usual instruction of this School'. The Committee decided to take him on trial for three months. It was not a success: they had to write to Bird's father and ask him to take the boy away, 'as he still continues to appear incapable to receive instruction'.

There was a change in the rules in 1809, the minimum age at which pupils were admitted was lowered from twelve to ten years. The first children to benefit from the new rule were two eleven year olds, Charles Johnson from Beighton and John Brittain from Honingham. Ten year old Jeremiah Hewson from Bixley followed in April 1810.

The Institution was not designed to be run as a prison of course, or even as a Workhouse. Rules on the movements of residents were laid down in

August 1806 but they were rather ambiguous. The first stated that no-one was to go out at all, except to a church service on Sunday afternoons. Another said that no-one was to be out after 8 pm, and that if they came back after 7 pm they would go without their supper. Yet another resolution took a different approach: no-one could go out at all unless someone came for them and promised to return with them. This rule was also qualified – patients *could* go out on their own if they were running errands for the Matron.

As with so many institutions, the diet, although adequate, was distinctly dull:

	Breakfast	**Dinner**	**Supper**
Sunday	Bread and Butter	Roast Meat, Potatoes and Dumpling	Rice Milk
Monday	Milk Broth	Suet Pudding	Bread and Cheese
Tuesday	Milk Broth	Roast Meat, Potatoes and Dumpling	Meat Broth
Wednesday	Milk Broth	Suet Pudding	Bread and Cheese
Thursday	Milk Broth	Roast Meat, Potatoes and Dumpling	Rice Milk
Friday	Milk Broth	Boiled Meat, Potatoes and Dumpling	Meat Broth
Saturday	Milk Broth	Pea Soup	Bread and Cheese

Even this limited variety compares favourably with that at Liverpool where 'boarders were fed on an almost identical breakfast and supper, of gruel or porridge and bread, throughout the year'.[2]

Who paid for the Norwich Institution? It received most of its money from subscribers, people who volunteered to give a set amount – usually between one and five guineas – each year. It also received benefactions – one-off gifts, very often legacies. The subscribers made up a significant number of the middle and upper class of the county. By 1807 there were over 2,000 of them. Of course some subscriptions would stop as the donors passed away, but other names would be added to the list: Philip Meadows Martineau subscribed two guineas a year from 1808 for example and Jeremiah Colman soon added his name to the list. Income from subscriptions remained fairly constant in the first decade of the nineteenth century, at about £400 a year.

Large benefactions in the early years included £100 bequeathed by Mrs Ann Wright in 1807, £525 from Mr Henshaw, a merchant of Oldham, in 1808, and £100 from Thomas Audley in 1809. In 1810 there was an anonymous gift of £400 and in 1811 John Lacon of Great Yarmouth bequeathed £200. Two years later R. Warmington left £500. Naturally the total amount received from benefactions would vary enormously. For the years 1807 to 1814 the amount given ranged from a mere £86 in 1812, to £775 in 1808. The average amount received in gifts in this period was just over £350 a year.

The donation from Henshaw was made on condition that the Institution was opened to the kingdom at large. The Committee unanimously resolved to do this. Henshaw also played a major part in another foundation, much closer to his home town. Held up by a lengthy legal dispute, the Henshaw's asylum in Manchester opened over twenty years later, in 1835.

The Institution also benefited from the will of Thomas Cooke, who died in 1811. Known as 'the Pentonville miser', he was an eccentric who had been born in Norfolk. He left £1,000 to the Institution: this was just one part of a total legacy of over £15,000 that Cooke bequeathed to seven Hospitals and Institutions in the county.

Audited accounts survive that show the money was carefully spent, with an eye to the future of the Institution. In 1807–8, £188 was invested in 3% consols, and three tenements adjoining the Institution were purchased for £210. The income for the rents of these properties start to show up in the accounts from 1808; just over £20 a year was collected, but there were occasional expenses for repairs and maintenance. By 1810 the Institution had £2,800 invested in consols, which gave an income of £85 in the following year. By 1811 the amount invested had gone up to £3,500: the income was always exceeding expenditure and it was being invested for the future. Even in 1811, the books were balanced despite unusually large bills from the carpenter and bricklayer: clearly major repairs or improvements were taking place.

The accounts for manufacturing products in these early years also survive, but are not very informative. Most figures refer to 'sundries bought' and 'sundries sold'. There are references to the buying of osiers, and the sales of produce, mainly baskets, brought in approximately £8 a month on average.

For the years 1810 to 1825 there is a detailed record of the pupil's weekly activities. George Langley, a 13 year-old boy from Great Massingham was admitted on 6th January, 1813. He was trained in basket making and began actually making them in January 1815. He normally made four to six baskets a week. The value of the materials he used was about two shillings a week and the baskets were sold for about four shillings, so that the Institution was earning about two shillings a week from his work. He was given a 'reward' every four weeks, usually of three or four pence. He had breaks of two weeks each Christmas and one week at Whitsun. Langley worked through until June 1817 when he was taken ill: he died on 29th June aged just seventeen.

Males admitted seem to have outnumbered females, sometimes by three to one. The only trade on offer for women and girls was spinning. One example is Ann Pitts of Banham, admitted on 2nd February, 1818 at the age of twelve. She started earning at the end of August 1820. Her efforts earned the Institution less than a shilling a week, and her monthly reward was usually just a penny or two pence. This was clearly all the Committee expected: she left on 21st February, 1821 'after having served her full time to the entire satisfaction of the Committee and the Matron'.

Not all cases worked out so well, of course. Thomas Frankfit, aged 14 and from Gravesend was admitted in 1817. He was taught to make mats and began work in April. However, he cut his fingers in his second week and again in August. He continued to make mats but suffered further damage to his fingers in 1820. The Committee decided that it was the wrong trade for him and he was retrained in basket making.

The economic situation of the Norwich Institution can be compared with a parallel one, that of St. George's Fields in Southwark. This had been founded in 1799, and of course was a training school with no provision for elderly blind. The President was the Bishop of Durham. There were 24 on the Committee including two clergymen. Income for the year 1815 included over £4,000 from subscriptions and donations and £220 from legacies. Contributions from parishes came to £235. Sales of articles made by pupils brought in £1,368. However, materials for making the articles cost £1,073. Other major expenses were £1,228 for provisions, £785 for salaries and wages, and £450 for clothing.[3]

The Norwich accounts for 1811 (the nearest year to 1815 for which they survive) show the similarities between the two institutions – and the differences in scale. Income from subscriptions at Norwich was £436, with over £450 from benefactions, mainly legacies. Fees from parishes brought in £80. The sale of articles raised just over £100 but the expenditure on raw materials and wages was over £240. Housekeeping expenses, including servants' wages were £557 and clothing cost £63.

The Southwark school was in fact the best-endowed in England and had the most pupils – 36 males and 26 females in 1814. By the 1830s it had over 100 pupils. Norwich was about half its size: in 1814 it had 25 pupils – but it also housed seven elderly residents.[4]

Many of the key players in the early years of the Institution continued to be involved for many years, a tradition of lengthy service that has been a feature throughout its history. Thomas Tawell himself died on 4th

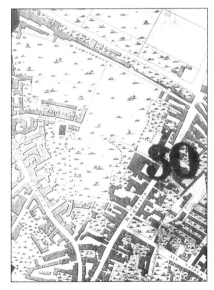

Map of the area, 1830

June, 1820, aged 57. He may have been ill for a while: a committee meeting was held at his house in the Close in April. However, he was able to attend a meeting at the Institution on 15th May; it was to be his last. He is buried in the Cathedral, appropriately within the chapel of the blind bishop, Richard Nix. The pupils were given a week off to commemorate the death of the founder. Mary Mountain died in August 1821 aged 72, and still giving her service as matron. In 1836, Mr Swan gave up his teaching role after 29 years of service. He was allowed a gratuity of ten shillings a week. Charles Ray was appointed as his successor at £20 a year, and at the same time Thomas Hammond was appointed to teach mat making at 14 shillings a week.

The new Poor Law of 1834 saw a change in the way that the inmates were supported. Parishes were grouped together into unions. Each union had a large workhouse into which all the people in receipt of relief were supposed to live – the unemployed, single mothers and their children, the elderly, and those with special needs such as the blind. However, the new unions could pay voluntary authorities to look after their blind, just as individual parishes had been doing. The usual figure paid to the Institution by a parish for looking after a blind person was three shillings a week. In practice, however, many of the blind remained in workhouses. The Blind institutions would not take children under the age of eight. They were also committed to training the blind: those found incapable of instruction would find themselves returned to the workhouse. The elderly blind had no specialised accommodation except at the Norwich Institution. They might be subsidised in their own homes or might be forced to live in the union workhouse: a national survey of 1861 found 593 long-term residents of workhouses who had been admitted because of blindness or defective sight.

In these years there were a dozen or so aged residents in the Norwich Institution, and about 30 pupils. There were slow but steady improvements in its infrastructure. A spinning ground was laid out in 1837. In the following year stockings were made for the first time, a sack-making department was established, and a stall hired in Norwich Market Place to sell the products made in the workshops. In 1841, a new building was erected for manufacturing sacks. It was 40 feet long and cost £250. In the 1950s it was still in existence being then used as the mat shop. From 1846 mats and rugs were also made: Giles Madge was appointed to teach these skills. Perhaps the Committee was slightly wary of him, noting at the time of his appointment that he was 'in no way to be considered an Indoor Officer of the Institution'. In 1838 the concept of journeymen was introduced. These did not live in the Institution but came in to work at making mats for which they were paid piece rates. There were four of these at first, all ex-pupils. By early 1839 there were twelve journeymen on the books of the Institution.

Dr James Alston, treasurer of the Glasgow Institution, visited the Institution on 30th April, 1839. Apparently on his advice, the Committee bought two looms and resolved to find someone who could teach sack weaving to the blind. At the same Committee meeting it was decided to hire a schoolmistress to teach reading and spelling. A Mrs Killett was appointed, at three shillings a week: she was to instruct the pupils in reading and spelling for two hours a day between Monday and Friday. The schoolroom was not a total success at first: in 1843 it was reported that the room was so cold that the pupils could not feel the embossed letters in their books. In December 1844 Barnard and Son offered to supply a stove for heating the schoolroom free of charge. This was turned down as Canon Thurlow, the Chairman, wished to donate a stove himself. A copper and range for the washhouse were ordered from Barnards instead.

In the 1840s, the books used in the school consisted entirely of books of the Bible. The school was run by lady volunteers who, in 1845, began to teach arithmetic as well as reading. The school meant that younger pupils than before might be allowed in. In 1844, for example, Ann Larkman aged six years was admitted as a pupil of the Reading School.

What forms of alphabet were used in the Institution? Many Institutions used a system invented by Thomas Lucas, a shorthand teacher in Bristol. It was intended to be both tangible and compact: the latter aspect meant that books produced in it were comparatively cheap, which no doubt helped it

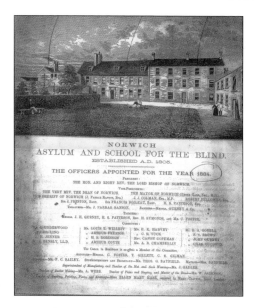

The buildings, 1845

to spread widely. Its main rival was an alphabet devised by the James Alston already mentioned. It was a Roman embossed type. In the summer of 1837, Alston wrote to all the blind institutions, advertising his version of the Gospel of St. Matthew. By 1840 the complete Bible was available in nineteen volumes and works of grammar and fiction had also been printed.

Another alphabet, that of James Frere, had received the backing of a London charitable society, which published the Bible and other religious works. It was introduced in Liverpool in 1838 but did not take off generally. In 1845, Frere's system was introduced to Norwich. The Committee was enthusiastic:

'The art of reading from embossed characters agreeably to Mr Frere's system has answered admirably. In the year 1843 Mr Frere spent some time in Norwich for the sole purpose of imparting his particular method of instruction to the Blind, and it was by his desire that the German Canons contained in the Sol-fa tune book have been expressed by characters selected from those employed for the purposes of reading. These characters are symbolical of the office belonging to each note in the scale, and by means of these the Blind are enabled to sing in Parts and instruct themselves in new tunes.'

The sol-fa system mentioned was a device for very simple musical notation. It was often known as the 'Norwich sol-fa ladder' as it had been developed by Sarah Glover, a music teacher in the city. A book explaining the system was published by Jarrold's in 1835. The Institution had direct contact with Sarah: in September 1843 she was asked to provide a 'harmonicon' for the use of the school.

The only blip in the good financial running of the Institution occurred towards the end of this period. In March 1843 the Committee decided they were unable to present a proper set of accounts. The Secretary, Mr Oldfield, appears to have had the monetary side of the Institution very much in his own hands but then committed suicide by cutting his throat, leaving financial chaos behind him.

Oldfield was buried at St. Paul's church in Norwich on 1st April, 1843. On 28th May, the secretary before Oldfield, Mr Addey, offered his temporary services to try to sort out the mess. Robert Cocksedge was appointed Secretary and Superintendent for a trial period of six months He was found unsatisfactory and was replaced by Edwin Yarington. The Committee decided to get rid of the Matron, Mrs Christopher, at the same time and offered a pension of £10 if she retired. She was replaced by Mrs de Carle.

In June 1843 the Treasurer had access to Oldfield's property: he found ten guineas in a small wooden box and almost £3 in a purse which he paid into the bank. He also found small sums of money belonging to five of the inmates and passed this money to the new Secretary. Oldfield's effects were sold for just under £15, not counting an organ estimated to be worth £20 'at most', which was retained by the Institution. Oldfield was reported to have had money in his hands for the year 1842 amounting to almost £100: the Committee was eventually able to get back £85 of it. There were similar occasional problems in other Institutions. In 1857 the Governor at Henshaw's, William Hughes, was forced to retire and in 1869 the Superintendent at Liverpool had to resign after accusations of extravagance. Since 1843, the Norwich Institution has conducted its financial affairs for over 150 years to the entire benefit of its inhabitants and without a hint of irregularity.

By 1846, the Committee felt that the troubles were over. The manufacturing department had been re-organised. An 'intelligent teacher' had been appointed in the weaving shop, which had led to great improvements in the rugs, sacks and matting. The Superintendent was now able to concentrate on the basket-weaving department. The school was also regarded as a success.

In 1850 the Committee considered the purchase of tenements for additional workshops, but eventually redeveloped and expanded the existing workshops at a cost of £200. The buildings on the south side of the Institution were bought in 1850 but put to other uses: one cottage was converted into a day room for the aged male inhabitants, thus giving them a separate space from the young men – 'an arrangement for which the poor men have expressed their gratitude'. The remainder of the new premises was rented out to raise further income.

The 1851 census was the first to count the number of blind, although no definition of blindness was supplied. The blind population in Great Britain was 21,487: one person in every 975 was blind. Just under 3,000 of the blind were under 20, and just over 10,000 were over 60. There were 379 blind people in England and Wales working as basket makers and 88 were working as mat makers. Over 400 were described as musicians but no distinction was made between those working in the streets and those in more 'respectable' lines of the business.

The 1851 census also gives us a snapshot of the Norwich Institution. The secretary was still Edwin Yarington. There were six live-in servants including a matron and a nurse: all of them were blind apart from the nurse. There were 13 elderly residents, five males and eight females. One lady was 40 years old but all the others were in their late fifties or older, including one of eighty. There were also twenty people described as 'at school': their ages ranged from twelve to thirty years old. Almost all the pupils and elderly residents came from Norfolk and Suffolk, with a few from Essex and just two pupils from further afield. Theodore Steggles, aged 17, was born in Basingstoke, and Edward Sykes, 22, was born in Middlesex.

Chapter 3

1855–1904

The 14th October 1855 was a Sunday, so it was decided to celebrate the 50th anniversary of the foundation on the Monday following. A holiday was granted, with cake and ale for lunch, tea at 6pm, and a dinner of roast beef and boiled legs of mutton, with plum and plain pudding and dessert. Tobacco was provided for the men and in the evening there was a concert for the residents and the subscribers. The residents and some of the journeymen played music and there was a display of work: 'several of the aged people and pupils expressed in suitable terms their thankfulness for the comforts they enjoy in the Institution'.

The second half-century of the Institution was to see a growth in both the school and the asylum, a major new building and, at the end of the period, a new development – a school for the elementary education of blind children.

In the 1850s there were further developments in the infrastructure. October 1855 saw the introduction of piped water and baths. The end of the decade saw a high level of illness, which was blamed on the state of the drains. The 1858 annual report said 'the past year has been one of great sickness; there have been more cases of illness than in any year for a long period'. The Committee blamed the insanitary nature of the site and took steps to improve the drainage. In 1863, gas was brought in for the first time at the end of the year. Pipes and burners were installed in the Hall, Sitting-Room, Schoolroom and kitchen at a cost of just under £6.

There was a minor domestic upset in 1856. Madge and the schoolmistress, Miss Wright, were accused of improper conduct. Madge was dismissed and Miss Wright resigned. An advertisement was placed in the local papers and circulated to the other Blind Institutions in the country:

> 'Two Officers wanted: A middle aged man competent to undertake the management of the Manufacturing Department, and to teach mat and carpet making; also a Schoolmistress, able to teach Reading (by Frere's system for the blind), Singing and Knitting.'

Thomas Gooch was appointed Superintendent at thirty shillings a week. Two candidates were interviewed for the post of schoolmistress and Marian Benson appointed: her salary was twelve shillings a week.

The annual report of 1870 looked at the progress made over the previous 65 years. It was still the only institution in the country providing both a school to train the blind and an asylum for aged blind people. It stressed that the school gave the pupils a sense of self-worth:

> 'It is perhaps difficult to point out any two situations in life more opposite to each other than the condition of a Blind person, with faculties benumbed by sloth, and spirits depressed by the consciousness of infirmity, and that of the same individual engaged in regular employment, and knowing that he or she contributes by daily occupation to the comfort of the family of which either forms a part.'

Pupils were encouraged to work by receiving small rewards in proportion to the amounts which they had earned for the Institution. A very wide range of goods was being made, some evocative of mid-Victorian England:

> 'The male pupils may be seen employed in making baskets, mats, matting, rugs, sacks and envelopes for packing wine bottles. The female pupils knit stockings (worsted and cotton), guernseys, socks, night socks,

gaiters, knee caps, gloves, gauntlets and driving gloves, antimacassars of every description, covers for cushions, ladies' and babies' shoes; they also make a variety of fancy wares in wool; some of the aged women sew and knit; and most of the boys make nets for fruit trees and other purposes, and occupy part of their leisure time in knitting and netting.'

The report also stressed the religious instruction given to the pupils: Mr Frere's books were still being used for scripture studies. Also in 1870, it was reported that 'an ingenious substitute for writing has been adopted, by which means pupils are able to communicate with their friends, and by a process somewhat similar to that adopted for writing, they are taught to work sums in arithmetic'.

In 1885, a blind man became Mayor of Norwich. This was John Gurney, the eldest son of John Gurney of Earlham. A banker by profession, Gurney became blind in 1881 when he was in his thirties. He proved a very active mayor, organising the building of a road over Mousehold Heath as an opportunity for unemployed men to have work: the road is now named after him. He also played a key role in transforming Norwich Castle Keep from a prison into a museum. As might be expected he took a special interest in the work of the Blind Institution. The Gurney family had been one of its most generous benefactors over the years: their gifts had included £50 from Samuel Gurney in 1839, £25 from Jane Gurney in 1840, and £500 from J. J. Gurney in 1843. It was usual for the current mayor of the city to attend the annual meeting of subscribers to the Institution. Gurney did this on 3rd June, 1886. His speech included the words:

> 'For the encouragement of the blind I can say that I consider my loss of sight has been amply compensated by other gains. Before, I did not so fully appreciate sympathy, while the moral good which has come to me has been infinitely greater than my material loss.'[5]

In 1886, John Shave and his wife were appointed as Superintendent and Matron. In this year there was a health crisis at the Institution, sixteen of the residents were infected with typhoid fever. The Committee

The buildings, 1882

sent most of the others to friends on a temporary basis. A house was rented in Greyfriars for those who had nowhere to go, and the Institution was thoroughly cleansed and aired. The Chairman, Canon Copeman, decided it was time for a new building. The current building had been a private house, to which various additions had been made over the years and clearly it was no longer adequate for its present purpose. Some people thought they should spend a part of their accumulated capital – which then amounted to £15,000 – on this. John Gurney wrote a letter on 30th January, 1887 suggesting this course and offering an annual subscription of £50 a year for life. Some subscribers thought a new building would be too large an undertaking and suggested merely refurbishing the old buildings. One, R. A. Gorell, pointed out that Gurney's offer was only one-ninth part of that money needed, and was in any case only for life. This last point was a valid one. Gurney was very ill and was staying in Cannes for the sake of his health: he did indeed die on 24th February, 1887.[6]

In the end it was decided to take the risk and put out an appeal to fund a new building, which would be large enough to house fifty people.

The architect Edward Boardman estimated the work would cost £5,000. In May 1888 the Earl of Leicester presided at a public meeting in Norwich to raise money for the new buildings. The Institution asked for £4,000 from the public and received no less than £5,500. The new buildings cost just over £5,320: the largest contribution was a legacy of £2,500 from a Miss Weston. In 1889, the Prince of Wales consented to be Patron of the Institution and allowed the Royal Arms to be placed over the entrance. He continued as Patron when he became King, and every sovereign since has also acted as Patron.

The new buildings, a long-lasting memorial to Copeman's chairmanship, were opened on 14 June 1890. A further appeal was launched to fit out the new building and to lay out the grounds. On 22nd January, 1891, the singer Lottie Lehmann gave a concert at St. Andrew's Hall and visited the Institution. The concert raised £158. Other major contributions included £200 from the Earl of Leicester and £150 from Gorell. The annual report listed over 300 subscribers ranging in order of

The new frontage along Magdalen Street, 1889

size of donation: last in monetary value, but not least in terms of love, was a gift of three pence from an unnamed little girl. The formal opening was on 16th October, 1891: it was led by Sir Joseph Savory, the Lord Mayor of London.

An account of the Institution made in 1890 tells us that Bible Instruction was being given by means of 'Doctor Moon's system', which used books with raised or embossed letters. The system had replaced those of Alston, Lucas and Frere. William Moon was a blind man and the principal of the Blind School in Brighton. His system used some Roman letters, altered so as to increase their tangibility, placed some at angles to represent other letters, and also a few arbitrary signs. The result was close enough to the Roman alphabet to be familiar to people once sighted and literate. The system was expensive to produce, but, as it became popular, bulk printing allowed prices to fall, especially as the system was energetically promoted by Moon himself and by the British and Foreign Bible Society.

However, the year 1890 also saw the first reference to the use of Braille in the records of the Institution. On 9th September the Committee ordered a quarter-stone of Braille paper. This is a system based on a series of embossed dots invented in Paris by Louis Braille: its basic form is like that of one half of a domino, with two rows of three dots. Sixty-four combinations of embossed dots are possible, more than enough for any European language. It has the great advantage that it can easily be written as well as read by the blind. It was the system favoured by the British and Foreign Blind Association after lengthy consultations with blind people in 1870. The Association sold books, music, writing and arithmetic frames and embossed maps and games. By 1890 the books offered included novels by Dickens, plays by Shakespeare and poetry by Tennyson.

By the First World War, Braille had become established as the predominant system. The Moon system did continue in a much smaller way, many people were used to it and did not want to change. It was also used more easily by elderly people who had lost the sensitivity in the fingers needed to read Braille at speed.

The Board Room

The regulations of the Institution were revised in 1891. The new rules for pupils and inmates were as follows:

The pupils shall rise in the morning at the ringing of a bell, at six o'clock in the summer, and seven in the winter; and shall commence work at seven o'clock in the summer, and nine in the winter.

The hours for meals shall be – Breakfast 8 am; Dinner 1 pm; Tea 6 pm; Supper 9 pm. The pupils shall cease from school or work at twelve o'clock and five o'clock. On Saturdays they shall not be employed in the workshops after twelve o'clock. When the bell has rung for bed, they shall proceed to their bedrooms in an orderly manner, taking off their shoes before going upstairs.

Smoking in unauthorised places, spitting on the floors, or the introduction of food or drink without permission, are strictly prohibited; nor are any of the pupils, on any account whatsoever, to meddle with their stoves, fires or lights.

Inmates found persistently idle, or wasting or destroying any material for work, shall be reported to the Committee.

Grace shall be said by one of the pupils, or sung before and after meals, and noisy talking shall not be allowed.

On Sunday, the inmates shall rise at seven o'clock, and after breakfast take quiet and orderly exercise till they go to church. Friends may take them out before or after dinner, till nine o'clock in the evening. The male inmates may go out on one Sunday, and the females on the next. Pupils will not be allowed to go out at any other time, except during the holidays, or by special permission. Such permission may be given by the Secretary under exceptional circumstances, which shall be reported to the Committee.

Holidays shall commence on the Wednesdays before Whitsuntide and Christmas; the summer holiday shall be four weeks and the winter holiday a fortnight.

The pupils shall not frequent public houses.

The journeymen shall cease from work at 1 pm and 6 pm, except on Saturdays, when they shall leave work at four o'clock in the afternoon.

The aged workers shall do any work they are capable of doing in the house, when required by the Secretary or Matron, and shall not leave the house except by permission.

The pupils are required at all times to be respectful, cleanly, and orderly. Improper language, or immoral or disobedient conduct, shall be instantly checked by the Secretary or Matron, and if persisted in, reported to the Committee.

The rules shall be read on the last Saturday in every month by the Secretary.

The Mat Workshop, about 1900

View of the Gardens

In 1893, George C. Eaton became treasurer on the resignation of J. Farrar Ranson. He took an active part in the welfare of the Institution: in 1896, he and his wife persuaded the actor Mr Bancroft to give one of his popular readings of the Charles Dickens' classic 'A Christmas Carol'. It took place in St. Andrew's Hall. The profits were split equally between the Institution and the Lying-in-Charity: each received almost £40.

Canon Copeman died in 1895. The annual report paid tribute to his work:

> 'He was indeed an ideal Chairman, and his impartiality, his calmness, his extensive knowledge, his almost unequalled experience in the affairs of our City, his judicial mind, all these qualities fitted him for the post of Chairman in a very high degree, in which very few men could compare with him.'

A major departure from Tawell's vision came with the establishment of an elementary school within the Institution. It proved to be a project with a short life. The Elementary Education (Blind and Deaf Children) Act of 1893 made it the duty of the local School Board to provide education for the blind and the deaf until they were 16. The Act defined blind scholars as those unable to read ordinary schoolbooks, so that only a minority of the new pupils were totally blind. The pupils had to attend a school certified by the School Board. Few School Boards set up their own schools, preferring to adapt the existing voluntary institutions. This was the case at Norwich. A new element was now added to the Institution: a school for elementary education. In 1895, the Blind Institution was inspected by the Inspector for the Norwich School Board and 'certified' under the Blind, Deaf and Dumb Act of 1893. Children from the School Board would be received as day scholars at £7 a year, or as boarders for £30 a year. In 1895 there were six boarders and five day-pupils.

In 1897 the Inspector visited again and reported that the pupils were being 'carefully taught'. In 1898 there were 24 children.

However, in 1898 the report was less favourable, stating that 'the standard of attainments was not high' and that the teaching department was not strong – and also that it was not desirable that meals were being taken in the same room as pupils were taught. In the same year Miss Hase resigned after 25 years as head teacher as she was to be married. She was replaced by Miss Hollway who had qualifications from St.

Ladies' Sitting Room

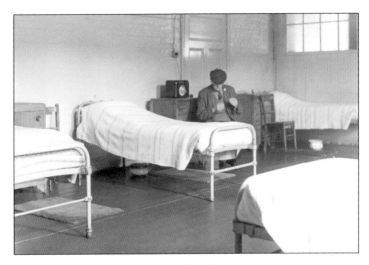

Men's dormitory

Andrews and Cambridge. She had been at Dr Campbell's Royal Normal College for the Blind in Norwood. The authorities also made a new appointment, Miss Helen Adams, as assistant mistress. She was unsighted and had worked for the Royal Normal College for nearly eight years. The annual report was enthusiastic about her: 'Miss Adams is well qualified to teach music, both vocal and instrumental, as well as type-writing and other things which may be needful to be taught to the blind'

(The Normal College had been established in 1871 under Francis Campbell, a blind American academician and music teacher. It filled a need by providing an academic and musical education for blind people rather than instruction in manual trades. Its pupils ranged in age from six to eighteen or over. In 1896, it was recognised by the Board of Education as a teacher training institution. Several of its pupils, like Miss Adams, went on to become teachers in blind institutions.)

By 1900, the Board of Education was demanding more from the Norwich Institution. It wanted separate departments for boys and girls and separation of the sexes out of school hours, as well as a new building for a schoolroom. They threatened to withdraw their certificate from the school. The governors estimated that it would cost £5,000 to undertake these works. They were losing £250 a year in providing education for

The Elementary School, 1890s

blind children and they decided to call a halt: the school would close on 31st March, 1901. A meeting of subscribers unanimously agreed. Norwich was not the only Blind Institution to find the concept of an elementary school unworkable: the governors at Plymouth also closed down its school.

The children were moved to another school provided by the Norwich School Board – Miss Adams went to the new school as a teacher. However, she continued to live at the Institution. In June 1902 she asked for a reduction in the twelve shillings a week she was being charged for board and lodging, as she could not get from Horn's Lane to have her midday meal in the Institution. She was having to pay to have lunch at the Cookery school and pay for it herself. The Committee saw the justice of her case and reduced the charge by 2s. 6d. In her place, Miss Williamson, again from Norwood, was appointed as teacher to the adult pupils in the Institution. Miss Adams returned to the Institution after the First World War and was still teaching Braille there forty years later!

In 1904, the various education authorities in East Anglia met and agreed to build a new school on the 'cottage home' plan. The problem was finally resolved in 1911 with the opening of the East Anglian School for the Blind and Deaf at Gorleston.[7]

The 1901 census shows just over 1,000 blind basket makers and over 150 blind mat makers in England and Wales, showing that the Blind

Basket and cane seat Workshop, about 1900

Institutions were successfully training up people to maintain themselves with these skills.

The same census also shows how the Norwich Institution had changed over the fifty years since 1851. There were a lot more residents – 58 in all. The superintendent was still John Shave, and his wife Clara still acted as Matron: their three young children lived with them. There was a teacher in residence, Helen Adams, seven female servants and one male servant: Helen and three of the servants were blind. There were 13 inmates, all in their late fifties and above. There was a real change in the character of the pupils compared with 1851. There were 30 of them and some were very young: the youngest female pupil was nine years old and one of the boys just seven. The origins of the inhabitants had not altered much, however, almost all were from Norfolk and Suffolk, with just a few from Essex. Only one from further away, nine year old John Thome, who had been born in Oxford.

As always, treatment of applicants and residents required sensitive decision-making. In February 1901, the case of Herbert Rebbeck, an inhabitant of Marlborough Workhouse was raised: he was both blind and deaf. The Committee wanted to know how he communicated with his fellows and by what means they communicated with him. It also queried how the Master of the Workhouse thought that Rebbeck was capable of being taught a trade. It is perhaps not surprising that at their next meeting the Committee decided not to accept Rebbeck. In January 1903 William Wilson was reported to the Committee for insubordination while engaged in chair caning. He was brought before them and said that he was unable to master the details of this handicraft and that he had been kept to this work for three whole months. He promised that he 'would try and do better'.

The closure of the elementary school meant that there was more space for non-resident journeymen. In 1902, there were 43 inmates of whom nine were journeymen. The Committee commented that they had 'ample accommodation for many more'. In 1902, £555 was raised from the sale of manufactured goods, mainly baskets (£303), and mats (£145). However, the costs were greater than the profits. The two main elements of these were the raw materials at £294, and journeymen's wages at £152. They must have been building up a stock of material: in the following year less than £3 was spent on it, so that a profit was made from manufacturing – albeit a mere £12.

In December 1902, the Institution received a legacy from Susannah Rump: this was of £108 in cash and £4,286 in stocks. The legacy also provided for an annual concert in the Institution. Susannah had died in 1896 having appointed the Institution as her residuary legatee. The will was disputed by the executors but upheld after lengthy legal proceedings.

The kinds of entertainment offered to the residents can be typified by those listed in the 1902 annual report. Colonel Patteson and his wife gave them a musical entertainment with a 'substantial supper'. Miss Bignold invited the residents to a Concert she gave in Noverre's Rooms. In July, Mr and Mrs J. H. Gurney entertained the inmates at Keswick Hall, followed by a country drive. There was another drive later in the summer and in October the inmates were invited to one of the evening concerts during the Triennial Musical Festival, followed by a supper. In December Miss Gorell provided a tea for all the inmates and in the same month F. R. Eaton provided the apparatus for a skittle ground 'which the male portion of the inmates much enjoy for purposes of amusement and recreation'.

Chapter 4

1905–54

The centenary of the Institution was celebrated in some style on 14th October, 1905. There was a special dinner or tea for the residents. 'By direction of the Committee all the meals throughout the day were made special'. In the evening a musical entertainment was given by the Reverend Precentor Moss and Miss Constance Copeman, assisted by other friends, both from within and without the Institution, together with the Norwich Orpheus Glee Party. A 'most successful and delightful evening was spent, a large phonograph, kindly lent by Mr George Green, adding to the variety and success of the occasion'. In this centenary year there were 55 'on the books'. Thirty-three were at the technical school, and there were thirteen elderly residents. There were nine non-resident journeymen. Sales of manufactured goods raised £656. Donations in the year were just under £62, legacies £138 (they had come to a mere 14s. 8d. the previous year!), and subscriptions brought in £276.

The third half-century was to see two world wars, both having a direct effect on the Institution, and a revolution in the treatment of the blind arising from the Blind Persons Act of 1920.

The 1905 Regulations show that the Institution had reverted to Tawell's original scheme of combining a training school with an asylum for the elderly:

1905 REGULATIONS

ELIGIBILITY

The Institution is open as a TECHNICAL SCHOOL for a term not exceeding five years (unless with a special permission from the Committee), to persons over sixteen years of age as pupils; and as an ASYLUM to persons of the age of fifty-five years and upwards.

The rule of the charity as to both these classes of application is that they must be totally blind; the Committee may, however, exercise discrimination in admitting cases where the applicant has some guiding sight. A contribution towards maintenance is required for each blind person admitted.

The payment to be made by Boards of Guardians, both in the cases of the Technical School and those of the Asylum is £18 4s 0d per annum; such amount having been sanctioned by the Local Government Board. The same will be required where the payment is made by private persons, unless the Committee shall consider that the circumstances justify some departure from the rule.

In neither class is it necessary that the blind applicant shall be a resident in Norwich or Norfolk, but preference will be given to the applications of such residents.

ADMISSION

In all cases, a Form of application must be obtained from the Secretary at the Institution, which must be properly filled up, as therein directed, and returned to the Secretary to be laid before the Committee for their consideration. This form contains:

1. Questions as to the age and circumstances etc of the blind applicant. The answers to the questions must be certified to be correct by a parent or guardian of the blind person, and by a minister of religion to whom such applicant is personally known; or, in the case of a Board of Guardians, by the Clerk to the Guardians of the district in which the applicant resides.

2. Questions to be answered by a Medical Man who has examined the applicant.

3. Questions to be answered by the Medical Officer of the Institution, who will also examine and report on all applicants thought suitable for admission.

4. A Form of Engagement for boards of Guardians, as to the payment of the amounts required, and the fulfilment of the other conditions of the agreement. A Form of Engagement of a similar character for private cases. (These forms must be stamped).

5. A list of clothing required to be brought by those admitted; and information as to vacancies etc.

6. Recommendation of the case to be signed by a subscriber.

By 1909 the number 'on the books' had risen to 63, but there were still only nine journeymen. In that year a total of £156 was raised from the sale of manufactured goods mainly baskets (just under £75) and mats (£45). However, a greater profit was now being made as costs had fallen dramatically. Manufacturing costs were just under £120, of which by far the greatest element was the journeymen's wages at over £50. The cost of raw materials was a mere £22. 8s.

The Blind Institutions as a whole had trained up a considerable body of workers by 1911. According to the census of that year, there were 1,100 blind basket workers, 186 mat makers, 138 knitters, and 223 brush makers. Over 500 blind people were engaged in music as a profession: no less than 103 as teachers.

In 1911, John Shave died: he had been Superintendent and Secretary for 25 years. He had been pessimistic about his future in his last years, feeling that his work had not been appreciated. Gordon Phillips transcribes a letter he wrote to the Liverpool Asylum: 'I have managed the Norwich Institution for the Blind now over 23 years and I am only getting the small sum of £60 per annum and my wife as Matron £40 per annum, and there appears to be no further chance of any advance for either of us, but here we must remain now to work as long as we are able to do so, and than finish up our lives in the Workhouse, that is all we have to look forward to in the end, there is no Superannuation, or Pension here to look forward to after all our strenuous work for the Blind (worse luck for us)'. In fact his fears were unfounded. Mrs Shave retired on a pension: she lived until 1944. Mr and Mrs Clements were appointed in their places.[8]

The Institution went through difficult years before the war with deficits in every year between 1909 and 1912. There was a surplus in 1913 after a special appeal had been made for the making of two fire exits. The Committee recognised the need to introduce up-to-date technology to keep its prices competitive. In 1912, two Harrison automatic knitting machines were purchased, followed in 1917 by round knitting machines. Sales reached £846 in 1913, but fell to £778 as a result of the outbreak of war in 1914: all garden fetes and sales of work were immediately cancelled. However, in the longer term, the war provided a great opportunity for sales of manufactured products. A new shop in Magdalen Street opened in 1915. It was formally opened by the Countess of Leicester on 27th July and took sales of over £15 on the first day.

Sales of products rose in 1915 to an all-time high of £1,033, and continued to rise throughout the war, reaching almost £1,900 in 1918. The Committee realised this was due, at least in part, to high prices in wartime, but pointed out that all departments were 'very fully occupied'. Sales continued to rise in 1920, but the post-war slump hit their income: sales fell by £700 in 1921 and fell further in 1922 and 1923. The corner was turned with an increase of £224 in sales in 1924. There was a

Staff, residents and pupils in the 1930s

general rise in sales in the 1920s and 1930s apart from a decline in 1928–30. In 1931 a new Basket workshop was opened at a cost of £2,000: sales rose by £555. In 1933 the equipment of the Mat Department was completely modernised.

The war caused changes in the life of the blind. Trench warfare and other battle situations in the First World War caused blindness in a large number of young men. A hostel for blinded soldiers and sailors was founded in 1915 by the National Institute for the Blind, the Red Cross and St. John's: it was called Saint Dunstan's. The men were trained in crafts, poultry keeping and market gardening.

The German army also suffered many blind casualties. In 1916 the German government began to train Alsatian dogs as guides for war-blinded soldiers. In the 1930s the concept spread to England: the Guide Dogs for the Blind was formed in 1934. The blind person and their dog are one of the standard images of blindness that sighted people have. However, a dog is only suitable for a minority of the blind: the person must be confident enough to follow the animal, and also have the space and resources to house and feed it.

The Institution suffered one direct fatality in the war. George Jarrold, who had been appointed clerk to the Institution in 1914, served in the Army: he died in October 1915 of wounds received when in action in the Dardanelles.

Concern about the treatment of soldiers blinded in the war led to the 1920 Blind Persons Act. County and County Boroughs had to draw up plans for the welfare of the blind; local education authorities had to provide technical instruction for the blind. These authorities could use charitable institutions and could give them financial support from the rates. They also had to compile a register of the blind in their area, but once again no scientific definition of blindness was provided by the Act. The definition it used was: 'so blind as to be unable to do any work for which sight is essential'. This was important as the old age pension of ten shillings a week currently given to everyone at the age of 70 was now to be given to blind people at the age of 50. In 1921 34,894 people were

Women's workroom

registered blind in England and Wales, of which 8,891 were entitled to receive a pension. By 1925, the number of registered blind had risen to 42,140 including 14,007 pensioners. The increase was due to a more liberal interpretation of what was meant by being blind, rather than to a growth in the number of blind people. For the same reason, the number of blind described as 'unemployable' rose from 46% in 1919 to 72% in 1929: these were people who had mental or physical disabilities in addition to blindness, and also those over 50 who had not been adequately trained for work.

The Gymnasium, about 1936

By agreement with Norwich City Council the Institute would employ all employable blind persons in the city who required it. Work would be in the workshops for as many as could be accommodated, others would be given work at home. The Council would provide a grant of £20 per person to augment their wages. A similar agreement was made with the Norfolk County Council in 1921 and with Great Yarmouth Borough Council in 1924. These councils would also give a grant of £20 in each case. In 1925 there were ten of these home workers. The idea spread beyond the Norwich and Norfolk councils: West Suffolk Council joined the scheme by the early 1930s and East Suffolk followed in 1937.

The Institution was formally registered under the Blind Persons Act. To suit the new times the name was changed too, from the 'Asylum and School for the Indigent Blind' to the 'Norwich Institution for the Blind'.

Delicate decisions were having to be made as always concerning potential and actual residents. Applicants in 1923 included William Saunders, 35, of Great Yarmouth, who 'had some sight and could distinguish light from darkness', and Albert Gibson who was 'totally blind in the left eye, and nearly blind in the right eye'. Both were admitted subject to the approval of the Medical Officer.

In August 1925 Ann Britt, 'age 82', was removed from the Institution to Norwich Workhouse Infirmary as her mind was demented. She had spent 72 years in the Institution. She died in the Workhouse after just four months: Her age this time is given as 87. In a reverse movement, 20 year old Agnes Slater was moved to the Institution from King's Lynn Workhouse in July 1926, as she was totally blind. Movement between institutions was not uncommon. Florence Newsome spent ten years in the Blind Institution, but was then found to be suffering from delusions: she was sent to the infirmary of her poor law Institution, Heckingham. However, by 1927 she had recovered and she returned to the Institution.

The case of Charlotte Cutting raised other issues. She was aged 19 years and eight months when she applied for admission in December 1924: she wanted to take a course in machine knitting. However, a resolution of 1919 prohibited the admission of anyone under 21 'on

Play 'The Willow Pattern' performed by blind girls

account of the difficulty of mixing the young people with the old'. It was decided to reduce the age limit to eighteen and Charlotte was admitted. Thanks to the new rules, 20 year old Lilian Stevenson, from Thetford, was admitted in August 1925.

Another difficult case was that of Elizabeth Townsend from Lakenham. She was only 21 but had already attended Blind Institutions at Gorleston and Nottingham: it was agreed that 'she could not learn much' but the Committee was willing to give her a three months trial as a non-resident pupil. Unfortunately she turned out to be incapable of instruction and was told that she had to leave on 23rd December, 1925.

Brush Workshop, 1936

The 1920s and 1930s saw some major improvements in the comfort of the residents. In 1925, the floors in the House were covered with linoleum: which 'will not only effect a great saving of work in the house but will also add largely to the comfort of the inmates'. A wireless set with a loudspeaker was installed in the Music Room: 'this has given much pleasure and is much enjoyed by the inmates'. Electricity was installed throughout the building in 1932, along with new lavatories for men, new baths for women and a new system of domestic water supply.

The same period also saw a new generation of people serving the Institution. In January 1925, C. R. A. Hammond was appointed to the Committee. In 1926 he became Chairman on the resignation of Colonel R. W. Patteson. The annual report was generous with its praise. In 1929, J. B. Youngs succeeded his father John Youngs on the Committee. A year later Mr Clements retired as Superintendent, to be succeeded by Mr and Mrs Fanthorpe. A new house was built in the garden for them: this made more room for the residents who now numbered 108. In 1932, a new basket workshop was erected at a cost of £2,000. It was dedicated to Henry Carter, who had died in that year. He had first joined the Committee in 1899 and was elected treasurer in 1900. On his death, his son, Oscar Carter, followed him onto the Board in 1932.

In the 1930s, the names of the subscribers were listed once more in the annual report, a practice that had been discontinued in the war. There were 149 subscribers in 1931–2. A direct appeal led to a rise to 178 in 1938–9. As always, the names included many of the most well-known families of Norfolk: Barclay, Colman, Eaton, Gurney, Jarrold, Jewson, Unthank.

The 1931–2 report stressed the progress made on the social side:

'A Troop of Girl Guides has been formed, and is registered as the 11th Norwich Troop, under the charge of Miss Patteson. Thirteen concerts have been held at the Institution and 19 invitations received for concerts etc in the City. Every type of game specially adapted for use by the Blind, such as embossed Playing Cards, Dominoes, Draughts, Chess

Opening of Brush Department, 1936

etc, are provided, and as will be realised the Radio Sets, pianos and Gramophone are a great attraction. Sighted readers, principally Toc H, come in daily, and Braille Magazines, Periodicals and Books are also provided. ... The Institution is most fortunate in having large grounds and certain sections are now being reserved for the use of Blind Residents who desire to take up a little gardening.'

In 1932 a temporary shop was opened in London Street, in premises owned by Barclay's Bank. This led to an increase in sales of goods, and also helped to raise the profile of the Institution in the city. In 1934 the Castle Meadow Blind Shop opened. This resulted in an immediate annual increase of sales of £1,242. In 1936–7 it was doubted if the profits would justify the expenses of the shop but this was a short-term problem. In 1954 sales from the shop came to £31,000: the products were made by 72 blind workers.

1934 saw a new brush workshop under the supervision of a fully qualified Foreman-Instructor. By 1935 it was already outgrowing the accommodation: 'the Brush Department has fully justified its inception and has now the largest turnover in the institution. It is in this department where orders from local Authorities are particularly appreciated. The new Workshop is proving ideal for its purpose and with the modern equipment and plant which has been installed, the

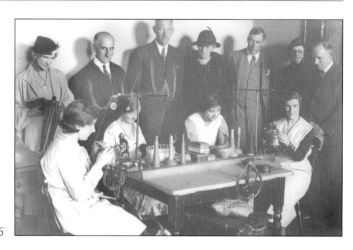

Civic visit, 1936

committee are able to offer full efficiency in every class of brush-making followed by the blind'. It was decided to build a new workshop with modern equipment. Contracts came in from the Admiralty, the War Office and local authorities. After the war the brush shop was rebuilt as the Knitting Department.

By 1936 the annual turnover was over £40,000, compared with only £3,000 in 1926 and £2,000 in 1916. Fees from Local Authorities brought in £6,000, but the main source of income was from dividends: £21,000 compared with a mere £800 a decade earlier and £600 in 1916. Annual subscriptions were a worry, having fallen to a mere £135, compared with £220 a decade earlier. A Special Appeal was launched in November 1936: this was advertised as being the first public appeal by the Institution for 50 years. The appeal pointed out that the Institution had begun in 1805 with just five people. Now, in 1936, there were 128 people on the books (not all residents, as we have seen), and this was expected to rise to 150 by 1940. The appeal explained the situation:

Some are fully trained Skilled Craftsmen earning their own livings. Other young men and women are being trained to become as skilful. Also we have a number of old men and women passing the evening of their days in quiet comfort.

Our activities are many: Knitting by hand and machine, Chair Caning, Mat Making, Brush Making, Weaving and Basket Making: we turn out 30,000 baskets a year.

Aeroplane rides, 1937

Growth in numbers has involved a large development of workshops and stores as well as living rooms. We still need room for old people and a Gymnasium for those who are younger in order to develop self confidence and physical fitness, which it is impossible for them to obtain by the usual exercises of sighted people.

Shut your eyes for half-an-hour and imagine you are blind and try to find your way about your own house. Think what it must be like. Picture to yourself your utter despair if you really were blind, and may the fact that the blessing of sight has enabled you to read this appeal prevail upon you to help us to brighten the lives of those who live in darkness, by teaching them a trade and providing them with work.

The appeal raised almost £8,000, including £500 from the executors of the late Doctor Sheppard Taylor. The total included the money from a radio appeal on 14th March, 1937 by Matheson Lang, which raised over £2,000. He and Jack Gladwyn, the proprietor of the Theatre Royal, donated the net profits from the first night's performance at the theatre on 26th April.

In 1938–9 there were 137 on the register. In the technical training department there were 22 residents and 10 day-pupils. Ten residents worked in the workshop: there were a further 42 blind people working there but living at home in Norfolk and another six coming in from Yarmouth. There were nine people working at home in Norfolk, and six in Suffolk. There were 31 residents in the home. In the same year a workshop and shop in Yarmouth, at 42, King Street, was opened so that the blind workers in the town no longer had to travel to Norwich.

In 1939 the shadow of war fell over the Institution. In July the Committee considered the question of air raid shelters, and also the situation of its employees under the Military Service Act. In November ten sighted members of staff went on an anti-gas course and the blackout was applied to the Basket and Mat Departments. In 1940 the town clerk took over part of the forecourt of the Institution to erect air raid shelters. Tenants occupying four cottages at the rear entrance asked permission to erect Anderson shelters on the Institution's property and this was agreed. In July 1941 more Anderson shelters were erected on land owned by the Institution.

Air raid precautions for the Institution's own residents consisted at first merely of outside trenches. Clearly this was most unsatisfactory, especially for the elderly residents and in winter. It was decided instead to strengthen the Concert Hall at a cost of £200. In April 1941, a Night Fire Watcher was appointed at a wage of £3 a week. In February 1942 the military authorities inspected parts of the premises with a view to possible military occupation.

War brings people together, the blind as much as anyone else. In 1941, the Cardiff Blind Institution was completely destroyed by enemy action. It appealed for assistance and the Committee decided to look into it further. At the same time a letter was received from the New York Institute for the Education of the Blind. It praised the 'spirit in which England was taking the war' and asked if they could provide any material help.

In the Second World War it was not just combatants who could be blinded. Between 300 and 400 civilians in England were blinded as a result of enemy action. The Institution itself suffered from enemy action. On April 27th and 29th April, 1942 the Baedeker raids struck Norwich

The Duke of Kent inspects bomb damage, 1942

and caused enormous damage as well as the loss of the lives of over 300 citizens. One 250-pound bomb fell on the Institution but landed in the garden. No one was hurt, but the knitting department was destroyed and the basket shop badly damaged. The roof was lifted off the main building and most windows were shattered. However, there was also a personal tragedy. On 27th April, Dorothy Jarvis, the Headmistress of the Institution, died in her own home at 41, Patteson Road, after the house suffered a direct hit. Her sister Beris and their mother and father were also killed. Dorothy was just 27 years old.

It was decided that workshop accommodation should have priority, followed by provision for pupils. Local Authorities were asked to take over responsibility for their Home Residents for the time being. The only suggestion the City Council could come up with was to use part of the Bethel Hospital in Norwich. The Committee was not happy, as this was itself in an area very likely to be bombed. In the end the elderly residents were evacuated to Burnham Hall.

Trading in 1944–5 reached an all time record of £18,075. Products included special airborne panniers 'of such help in assisting the various Air-Borne operations'. The Home also supplied thousands of baskets for potato pickers throughout East Anglia, and road scavenger brooms used

The Duke leaving the Institution

Workshop, 1944

by road sweepers throughout the area. Government contracts came to an end after the war but orders for brushes and doormats continued.

After the war, in 1946, twenty-four aged blind were brought back from Burnham Hall and the air-raid shelters in the garden were filled in.

Mr and Mrs Fanthorpe left in 1945: he had been appointed Master at the Great Hospital. The annual report summed up his achievement:

Floral gardens, 1947

The Queen at the Sandringham Show, 1947

'He was largely responsible for bringing the Institution up to date, so that we became the recognised training Centre for the whole of the Eastern Counties. He saw the building of our modern Basket and Brush Workshops, both of which were destroyed by Enemy Action, and had worked out plans with the Architect, to rebuild those and also plans for a new Women's Workroom and a new House for old people and many other improvements. His services and those of Mrs Fanthorpe who was for some years Matron, were invaluable, and we should like to place on record our appreciation of their services, and wish them every success and happiness in their new work.'

Basket Department, 1948

They were succeeded by Mr and Mrs Ledger, who came to Norwich from Warrington: 'he brings with him new ideas and enthusiasm, and the Committee feel the institution will continue to progress and expand its activities under his management'.

In June 1946 it was resolved to buy an Austin 8 van for delivering goods. In the end a Ford 8 utility van was bought for £375. Two years later a newer model replaced it. Houses were also purchased for members of staff. In 1946 a house in Chamberlain Close was bought for £1,500 to be occupied by Miss Cavan, the new Supervisor in the Knitwear Department. A second house, in Harvey Lane, was bought for the use of the assistant Secretary, Mr Webb. Another house was bought for the new foreman in the Basket department; this, a bungalow, was in Beechwood Drive, Thorpe. However, in 1948 the supervisor decided to move to a larger house. Beechwood was put up for auction, but withdrawn at £1,600. It was then sold for £1,750 by private treaty. In 1950 Miss Cavan moved to London to look after her mother and it was decided to sell the house that she occupied.

The workers went on strike for half a day on 4th June, 1947: this was after two of them had been discharged for being rude to the Matron and Assistant Matron, alleging that they were not being given sufficient food. The matter was speedily resolved, with the two men continuing to work at the Institution but living elsewhere.

The Putting Green,
1951

Immediately after the war it was decided to set up social centres in North Walsham, Caister, King's Lynn and Diss in co-operation with the local authorities: tea and entertainments would be provided. These centres were a huge success. In 1948, a new centre was established in Fakenham. Meetings were held once a month at each centre. They were very much appreciated by blind people scattered throughout rural Norfolk, who could very easily feel isolated and trapped in their homes. There was already a Blind Workers' Social Club in Norwich, in Catherine Wheel Opening, St. Augustine's. It had opened in 1944. In 1948–9 it was taken over by the Institution and was renamed the Norwich Social Centre for the Blind. It was open to all blind people in Norwich and the Committee estimated it would cost up to £1,000 a year to run. In fact they were spending £900 a year on the club in the 1950s, rising to £950 in the early 1960s.

Outings were being organised in the post-war years too, not just for residents but for other members of the blind community. They usually went to Yarmouth, but sometimes elsewhere: in 1947, 200 of the city blind were taken to Sea Palling in half a dozen buses: tea and musical entertainment was provided at Temple's Holiday Camp. The workers in the workshop also had an annual outing: in 1947 they went to Felixstowe.

The Sports Field, 1952

The 1952–3 annual report drew attention to the recreational facilities on offer:

'The excellent playing field on the south side of the Institution is used by many of the younger residents for football; a nine hole putting green has been laid out on the north side for the Institution's resident sighted staff, and it is pleasant to note that many of the blind people with some degree of sight are able to play during the lunch hour period. These coupled with the beautiful gardens, comprising about 5 acres is a surprise and delight to people visiting the Institution for the first time, coming as they do from the main entrance in Magdalen Street, which is so narrow. The flower baskets filled with geraniums now permanently attached to the front of the building itself, have beautified the building out of all recognition, and during the year the Prince of Wales Coat of Arms in stone and red brick has been faithfully reproduced in true colours of gold leaf, yellow and blue, together with the date in similar colours.'

The National Assistance Act of 1948 repealed the Blind Acts and increased still further the role of the local authorities. They had to provide information, instruction at home or elsewhere, workshops and hostels, work, assistance in marketing goods, and recreational facilities.

The shop on Castle Meadow, 1954

Many people thought that the National Health Service Act and the National Assistance Act meant that there was no longer a role for the Institution, or that its work would now be funded by the Government. In every annual report in the late 1940s and the 1950s, the need for continued support was emphasised:

> 'We wish to emphasize *we are still a charitable Institution relying upon voluntary subscriptions, donations and legacies.* We feel sure the present generation will not fail to bear the responsibility of providing funds to carry on the great work of providing for the blind, which is one of the few remaining voluntary organisations, that has not been nationalised. *We rely more than ever on the generosity of the Public for our very existence.* Every effort is being made to increase the number of Subscribers, *and to those about to make a Will, this Charity is most worthy of consideration. We are one of the oldest Charitable Institutions in Norfolk, and the fifth oldest Blind institution in the British Isles.*'

Chapter 5

1955–2005

The 150th Anniversary Dinner was held on 14th October, 1955. Roast Norfolk chicken was the main course, with peaches and cream and cheese and biscuits – and at the end of the meal 'cigarettes and coffee'. The Queen sent a telegram of congratulation and on 29th May, 1956 the Duchess of Kent paid a visit.

The Annual Report summed up the work that was being done. There were fifty elderly blind people resident in the home. There were 16 resident workshop employees, and a further 57 people worked there but lived at home. There were ten home workers in Norfolk, Cambridgeshire and West Suffolk. There were also three resident pupils in the Technical Training Department. No less than 17 local authorities were supporting these people, and the three trainees were supported by the Ministry of Labour and National Service. The trainees were being taught the crafts of basket, brush or mat making. The training took two to four years and after it the pupil might well transfer to the workshops: no less than six had done so the previous year. The departments of basket making, brush making and mat making all reported increased sales. Subscriptions were bringing in £150. Donations in the year were £875 and legacies £1,715.

The fourth half-century of the Institution was to see dramatic changes. The training and manufacturing side of Tawell's vision came to

59

an end. It was replaced by an enormous increase in the outreach work to blind and partially sighted people throughout the county. It also saw the development of a large network of volunteers who began to overcome the isolation of the blind from the sighted community.

For the first decades, however, manufacturing continued to flourish. A new mat shop was opened in December 1955: it had cost £8,000. The Institution was given the contract for fitting out Curl's new department store in Norwich, and also supplied many schools. Knitwear was slightly less encouraging. Goods were sold at the Castle Meadow shop under the trade name 'Blindmaid': 'it is beautifully made in the latest shades, distinctive in appearance and is most excellent value for money, and you will be helping our blind people to full employment by purchasing from us'. By 1962, the trademark was 'Blind Maid' but still sales were disappointing: the annual report blamed the craze for knitting at home – 'undoubtedly the British Women's most popular hobby'. In 1968 the trade name of workshop products was changed. Until then they had been marketed under the name of the 'Norwich Institution for the Blind'. The annual report said that 'it was felt that this carried with it an atmosphere of charity, whereas the workers are anxious to stand on their own two feet and to endeavour to compete freely with open industry'. The Committee decided to change the trading name to 'Norwich Industries for the Blind'.

The smallest department in 1955 was that of chair caning: the trade provided employment in slack periods in the knitwear department. The antique dealers, Bretts of Norwich, had used the Institution's skilled employees to re-cane reproduction and period chairs, some of which had been exported to America.

A new brush shop was proposed in the early sixties and an estimate for £12,256 was accepted in 1961. The Ministry of Labour agreed to pay one third of the cost. The final go-ahead was not given until 1964, by which time the estimated cost had risen by a further £1,000. However Sovereign Securities then offered £20,000 to buy the grassland adjoining the Odeon cinema car park, which was where the brush workshop was intended to go: indeed the builders, R. G. Carter, had already put up a

*The Duchess of Kent being greeted by
the Chairman, 29th May 1956*

workman's hut there. This led to discussion as to the future of the
Institution. The possibility of moving to a new site was considered but
rejected. It was also thought that as Magpie Road was redeveloped the
main entrance to the Institution could eventually be from there rather than
from Magdalen Street. In the meantime a new site for the brush shop was
found, away from the land Sovereign wanted. The land was sold.

Some members of the Committee saw the end of traditional trades
coming fairly soon. The possibility of making boxes was looked into: it
would, however, have cost £20,000 to buy the necessary equipment. At
this date (1964) there were 139 blind people from 20 local authorities on
the books. Over 80 were workshop employees. The whole of the building
along Magdalen Street was no longer adequate or safe and the Committee
began to consider the idea of a new purpose-built hostel. This would leave
the buildings along Magdalen Street empty – a useful financial asset for the
future. The new brush workshop opened in January 1965.

The Younghusband Report of 1959 and the Seebohm Report of 1968
both thought that work should be provided for all handicapped people

rather than for a specific group such as the blind. The Seebohm Committee saw the role that voluntary organisations could play in bridging the gap between the blind and the sighted. As June Rose wrote in 1970: 'There are of course social activities arranged, but they are very often for the blind, not with the blind. Now that the bare existence of blind people is assured by the state, surely the voluntary organisations can concentrate more on improving the quality of the life they live. And the kind of life people live depends largely on human contact'. The Norwich Institution had already developed along these lines and it was to do so with ever increasing strength in the last three decades of the twentieth century.[9]

A hostel for resident workers opened in August 1970, and a workers' canteen in the same year:

'With the completion of the Workers' Hostel the canteen, modern workshops and the landscaping of the surrounding gardens, we now have a blind community near to the city centre and one of which we can be justly proud. And so 1970 marks the end of a most exciting era of planning and final completion of a great act of faith.'

In fact, this was to be the height of the period of the workshops. In 1969–70 the two Knitting Departments (round knitting and flat knitting)

Residents in the garden, 1956

were closed. The workers were transferred to assembly work in the sub-contract department. This new department undertook engineering work under contract to local firms. By the end of the year sixteen men and women were working, and contracts had been secured with seven or eight local firms. Another innovation was to employ sighted disabled workers in the factory along with the blind workers.

A new department was established in 1971: the old established firm of Norwich Premier Wire Works closed and the Institution was able to purchase the goodwill, equipment and stock in trade of the business which was housed in the old knitting department. The home workers had fallen to just two, Mr Carrington in Holt, and Mr Burgess, a basket maker in Lowestoft. By September 1973 both men had retired, and the tradition of support for home workers came to an end. In 1974–5, sales for the sub-contract department came to £13,450 and the wire working department was employing ten men. However the more traditional trades were continuing to flourish: the making of baskets, brushes and mats employed 30 men and raised over £60,000 in sales in the same year. In 1974, the shop in Castle Meadow closed. The main outlet for sales was now the stands that the Institution ran at two shows – the Royal Norfolk Show and the Sandringham Show.

The Institution van, 1957

The last Technical Training Department pupils left in 1980, followed by the last residents in the Workers' Hostel three years later. In 1985 the Workshops were sold for £101,000. After 175 years one half of Tawell's dream – that of providing training for blind workers had come to an end. This led to the further development of aspects of the care of the blind not included in Tawell's vision, provision of facilities on the site for the non-resident blind, and also outreach to the blind in their own homes throughout the county.

The quality of the sheltered housing for the elderly developed rapidly over the half century. In May 1956 Mrs Owen, the daughter of Canon Copeman, wrote that she would like to make a gift in memory of her father's work. It was decided to build a new canteen for the residents. In 1964 Miss Helen Kennett transferred investments worth almost £30,000 to the Institution in memory of her mother, brother and three sisters. The money was to be used for the benefit of the resident elderly blind.

In November 1965, the first steps were taken to erect a modern purpose-built home for the elderly. Six architects competed for the contract: the winners were the firm Skipper and Corless. The target of the appeal was £30,000: over £23,000 came in. Over 1,000 people made contributions, including an anonymous gift of £2,000. Children in no fewer than 42 Norfolk schools raised money and a seven-year old boy recorded only as 'Paul' gave 15 shillings. The remainder of the money

A corner of the Reading Room, 1958

came from the capital fund. The new building was named Thomas Tawell House. By the end of 1968, thirty-five elderly blind were housed here. On 29th April, 1970, Princess Alexandra formally opened the new Home.

The Magdalen Street property was sold to a building developer for £30,000 in 1971: he planned to pull down the old buildings and put up shops and single-person flats, originally intended primarily for students at the University of East Anglia. The sale was complicated by the fact

Opening of Thomas Tawell House by Princess Alexandra, 29th April, 1970

Mat Making Department, 1958

that a small part of the property being sold was old church land: the deal was finally completed in November 1972. The Coat of Arms on the old building and the lists of subscribers on wood in the old boardroom were retrieved before the sale. It was also suggested that a plaque be put up on any new building marking it as standing on the site of the original premises of the Norwich Institution for the Blind.

A new project was announced: the provision of flats for elderly blind people who might need some help, but who did not wish full hostel accommodation. This took some years to fulfil and was expanded to thirteen sheltered single flats, together with a new administrative block. The overall cost was to be £245,000. The project was named Hammond Court and opened in May 1980. By 1984 several tenants had moved from Hammond Court to Thomas Tawell House as they became less self-sufficient. This was intended from the beginning: it meant that they could remain within the Institution and maintain contacts with people they had come to know.

Management of the factory was taken over by the local authority in April 1979. This meant the re-housing by the Council of the workers formerly in the hostel. It was decided to use the space to build more flats as there was already a waiting list of six for the Hammond Court flats. In 1986 the block was completed, with three double and four single self-contained flats for residents able to care for themselves. 'Many details of the flats were planned with guidance from the people who now live there, including the positioning and colour of the guide rails so that they blended in with the building to make it 'more like home' than a sheltered housing complex for the blind'.

There were continual improvements to the conditions in Thomas Tawell House. Double glazing was added in 1986. A dining room extension was completed in December 1990 – just in time for the traditional Christmas Party. In 1995 legacies were used to further modernise Thomas Tawell House: a new roof was built, there was an increase in the number of en suite rooms, and new bathrooms and new lavatories were installed.

A section of the Chair Re-caning Department, 1958

In May 2000 the new Bradbury Wing of Thomas Tawell House was opened formally by Princess Alexandra and Sir Angus Ogilvie. It is so-called in honour of the Bradbury Trust, who contributed almost £400,000 of the money needed. The Wing has twelve large bedrooms, each with its own lavatory and shower. Twelve residents moved in to the new rooms: this enabled the remaining rooms in Thomas Tawell House to be refurbished and to be made en suite.

Some of the most dramatic developments of the half century came in the field of outreach. There was an enormous expansion of this work between 1955 and 2004. The social clubs continued to expand. In 1968/9, the cost of running the Norwich Social Centre was £1,705 but Norwich City Council were contributing £1,314. In the mid 1980s, the contribution of the NNAB to the club was £495 a year. In 1991/2, £6,323 was spent on 16 clubs, with the Norwich Social Club receiving by far the largest grant, £1,250. In 1992/3, the amount spent on the clubs rose to £7,330 but, due to a change in accounting practices, the sums given to individual clubs no longer appear. The Norwich Social Club was open almost every day, and the Friendly People's Club met in the same building. Three clubs were meeting at the Vauxhall Centre in Norwich, including the Rainbow Club for the Deaf/Blind. There were also clubs in Acle, Broadland (meeting in

Brush Making Department, 1958

Sprowston), Dereham, Diss, Downham Market, Fakenham, Hunstanton, Lynn, North Walsham, Swaffham, Thetford and Great Yarmouth.

In 1988, the name of the Institution was changed for a second time: the idea had often been discussed in the past. The name 'Norwich Institution for the Blind' had become unappealing and incorrect. The word 'Institution' gave out a Victorian image, and the word 'Norwich' failed to express the fact that the organisation helped the blind throughout the county of Norfolk. It was giving grants to nineteen social centres and clubs throughout the county, from Lynn to Yarmouth and from North Walsham to Thetford. The new name was 'The Norfolk and Norwich Association for the Blind'.

Day trips for the blind community had been organised by the Institution since the Second World War. Week-long holidays for the blind were started in 1971: Forty reservations were made at a Lowestoft hotel and more in Gorleston. Each blind person would pay £5 with the Institution paying the rest of the costs including travel expenses. At first the response was disappointing but eventually almost all the bookings were taken up and the holidays became a regular feature of the Institution's programme. After the first year the £5 charge was revised to include both the blind person and a helper. This policy of extending the scope of welfare for the blind beyond the residents of the Institution marked a new direction, and one that was to expand enormously in the next quarter century.

In a further development, a Resource Centre opened in a temporary building on 22nd May, 1985. As the annual report says, it 'displays aids and appliances to help visually handicapped people with their daily living skills and any article in the RNIB catalogue can be obtained through the Norwich Institution for the Blind. A loan service for a large number of items such as writing equipment, watches and clocks, is available. Many of the smaller items are purchased from Charity funds and given free to visually handicapped people. Those who are newly registered and visit the centre are given several items, such as large print telephone dials, pension book guides, liquid level indicators and so on'. A permanent Centre was opened in 1989.

Also in 1989, five people were appointed as Community Workers, one for Norwich and the others to cover the county. Four more were appointed in 1990. The Association was now pro-active: it wrote to newly registered blind and partially sighted people offering help, and the Community Workers visited the social clubs and individual homes. They had their work cut out: there were 4,200 blind and partially sighted people in Norfolk. Activities now included sailing at Neatishead, swimming at the Norwich Sports Village, yoga classes in Great Yarmouth, and holidays. The answer was to build up a community of willing volunteers to help. A Volunteer Co-ordinator, Pauline Simper, was appointed in 1992 and within a few years there were 120 volunteers. One group of twenty volunteers was established to visit the five hospital eye clinics in the county to give support and advice to patients.

Holidays to the Norfolk coast had long been on offer. In the 1990s holidays further afield were also undertaken, including trips to Benidorm and, in 1997, to the Holy Land: the latter group was led by Rachel Simper and the party was made up of ten visually impaired and eleven sighted people.

Pauline Simper also produced the *Magpie News*, a quarterly newsletter that goes out free to every one of the blind and partially sighted in Norfolk. It was produced in large print, on tape and in Braille. In 1992/3, a new format for the annual report was begun, with a much

Single bedroom,
Thomas Tawell
House

brighter feel, including photographs, and also including information useful to the blind and their carers, such as details of the social clubs throughout the county, and lists and contact details for the talking newspapers in Norfolk. There were ten of these run by over 600 volunteers. The most popular was *Chatterbox*, covering the Norwich area and having over 800 listeners. Others included *Grapevine*, covering the Great Yarmouth area, and the *Mardler*, produced in Aylsham and covering North Norfolk.

Legacies were a key income stream, but the amount received would fluctuate wildly from year to year varying in the 1980s and 1990s from under £20,000 in one year to £460,000 in another. In 1995, the Association began to extend its funding beyond donations and legacies. Susanna Burr was appointed as part-time fundraiser. She had soon raised sufficient money for the purchase of a mobile Resource Centre trailer to take the services of the Association into the county. The trailer had a wheelchair lift, and included a counselling area, a computer area, a daily living equipment area and a kitchen area. In April 2000, a charity shop was opened in the Magdalen Street property.

A large legacy from Miss Constance Allen enabled the Association to buy back part of the old workshops and establish the Allen Centre, which is used for offices and for training. The extra space allowed the

*Double bedroom,
Thomas Tawell
House*

Association to expand its activities. A team of visually impaired volunteers act as 'telefriends' to isolated and lonely blind and partially sighted people throughout the county. Information days are held here for newly registered people in the Norwich area.

One way of making the public aware of the Institution has been by having stands at the Royal Norfolk Show and the Sandringham Flower Show. The Institution has been involved with the latter from its very beginning. The first Show was held in September 1866, and the Institution was one of the charities among whom the profits were distributed. The Shows were also good places to sell products made by the blind. More recently The Queen Mother was a regular patron, purchasing socks, baskets and other items at the stall. As we have seen, the Institution ceased to make and sell produce and for a while stopped attending the Sandringham Show. However, it began to run a stall there again in 1996. It has proved an important attraction at the Show, receiving regular visits from the Queen Mother and, after her death, from Prince Charles and the Duchess of Cornwall.

Sailing has continued to be a very popular activity. On 1st July, 1993, Princess Anne visited the sailing centre at Neatishead and met some of the blind sailors. Other sporting activities include tandem riding, with one sighted and one visually impaired person on each machine. In July

Sandringham Flower Show, 1997

1998, a 'tandathon' was organised a four-day event covering a large part of the county: one of its greatest supporters was Bruce Bursford, a world record-breaking cyclist: sadly, he died in a road accident the following year.

Other present-day facilities include Resource Centres in Norwich, King's Lynn and Great Yarmouth and temporary centres in Cromer and Diss, with a Mobile Resource Centre travelling to the smaller towns and villages. These centres offer information, advice and help. In 1997–8 for example, the mobile resource centre covered 7,000 miles and visited some 700 blind and partially sighted people in 45 locations throughout Norfolk. A team of community workers supports people in their home throughout the county. Trained volunteers visit Norfolk hospital eye clinics and offer information to patients about services available to visually impaired people.

Thomas Tawell House and gardens, 1993

As always, some of the people involved in running the Institution in the second half of the twentieth century had put in many years of devoted service. C. R. A. Hammond died in February 1959. He had been Chairman for 32 years. The Annual Report paid him this tribute:

> 'Mr Hammond was a member of one of East Anglia's greatest banking families, going as far back as 1770, who found time in an extremely busy life to give service to the hospitals and many other organisations, but particularly to this Institution in which he became interested in 1924 when he joined our Committee, after which he was appointed Chairman two years later. He was for many years too a Trustee of the Great Hospital, Norwich, and in the words of the Right Reverend Lord Bishop of Norwich at his memorial service at Sprowston parish church: "He gave himself completely to whatever he took in hand, and by his care and enthusiasm he made this Institution probably one of the best in the country". The Blind and Staff of the Institution have lost a true friend indeed.'

The tradition of family service is shown in the fact that Hammond's son joined the Committee to fill the vacancy caused by his father's death: he was immediately appointed Vice Chairman. This tradition continues to the present day. Richard Gurney, a present Trustee, is a member of

Flat knitting Department, 1981

the Gurney family which has given service to the Institution since its foundation. Mrs Robin Eaton, who was Chairman for nine years until 2003, is married to Tom Eaton: five generations of the Eaton family have played a major role in the work of the Institution.

Sadly, two members of stalwart family supporters died before the completion of the major rebuilding works of 1965–70. H. W. Back of Hethersett Hall died in November 1968. He had been a committee member since 1928, and was Chairman between 1958 and 1966. J. B. Youngs died in the same year. K. B. C. Riches, the Chairman, died suddenly in January 1976: he had served the committee for 24 years as Treasurer, Vice Chairman and finally as Chairman, which post he took up on the resignation of H. W. Back in 1966. Long-serving people who retired or died in the early 1990s included Sheila Thackeray who retired as Director in July 1992. She had joined the Association when she left school and worked for it for more than 40 years. R. W. Grimsay retired a year later. He had served the Association for 42 years, having been Superintendent and Secretary from 1964, Vice Chairman for three years, and Treasurer for eleven years. Humphrey Back died in 1994. He was on the board for over 20 years and had been Chairman between

Norfolk Lavender, Heacham, 1999

1979 and 1982. 'Sam' Hornor died in 1998. He was on the Board of Management for 37 years and Chairman from 1986 to 1989. His father, Mr Bassett Hornor, had himself served the Association for almost half a century. More recent trustees have maintained this tradition of longevity of service. Kevin Oelrichs has been a Trustee since 1976 and been both Chairman and Vice Chairman, Richard Harrison has been a Trustee since 1982 and Vice Chairman.

The 'Institution' has seen many changes in the 200 years since it was founded by Thomas Tawell. It has been able to adapt to the changing needs of the blind community that it serves. The element of sheltered housing for the elderly remains. The training school for blind workers has gone. Instead the Association, as it is now called, places much more emphasis on reaching out to the blind and partially sighted in their own communities throughout the county of Norfolk. Thomas Tawell and the eight generations of Norfolk people who have supported the Association

75

The Sailathon, 2000

over the last two centuries would undoubtedly have applauded the achievements so far. Now is the time for present and future generations to build upon their work and continue and develop their proud tradition of help and support to the blind in Norfolk.

Chapter 6

The Future

By John Child

The Scheme approved by the Charity Commission and sealed on the 1st November, 1983 stated that 'The object of the Charity should be the relief of blind and partially sighted persons primarily, not exclusively, resident in Norwich or elsewhere in Norfolk in such ways that the Board thought fit'. Basically these were the provision of accommodation and care, the provision of a community visiting service and the provision of educational and recreational facilities. These aims were wide ranging, well thought out and have stood the test of time, enabling the Association to make considerable progress over the years for the benefit of the approximately 16,000 people in Norfolk who have poor sight. I believe it is in the evolution and development of the existing services provided by the Association that the future of the Association lies and not in making any dramatic changes.

After the rebuild and redevelopment of the late 1990s, Thomas Tawell House now has 36 out of its 37 rooms fully en suite, providing first rate accommodation which, coupled with excellent well trained staff, means that the Association provides a residential care home of the highest quality and one that we are all proud of. As part of our service we also need to provide respite care and day care, both to give carers a break and, for those that receive the care, encouragement and stimulation.

NNAB representatives at the Buckingham Palace garden party, 2002

The sheltered or supported housing of Hammond Court has tenants ranging from 22 to 96 years old and encourages them to live independent lives, though help is available via Wardens, if necessary.

Looking to the future the Association needs to develop intermediary care between Thomas Tawell House and Hammond Court where different levels of care and help could be provided. This is very much the Government's present thinking and should not be ignored.

The establishment of the Resource Centre, now called the Equipment and Information Centre, and the introduction of outreach workers in the middle and late 1980s was a brilliant innovation by the Association. The way this has developed means that the Association now takes services out into the County to help the some 16,000 people in Norfolk with poor sight.

This outreach service remains one of the key elements of the future work of the Association. Support is going to be increasingly needed as more people retire to Norfolk; for example, sadly a husband often dies first, leaving a blind wife living in social isolation, knowing nobody, far

Marion Sweeney with award for 30 years service, 2002

George Bailey putting together the Magpie News, 2003

from family and friends. The Community Workers give valuable support and encouragement and enable people, many of whom now live longer, to maintain their independence at home.

As one of the Community Workers said in her report to the Trustees in 2002 'Our role is a vital link to information, knowledge and other supporting services. We are an informal, but informed, service offering skills from practical support to emotional support' and as a daughter said of another Community Worker in a letter to me 'I am sure you will already be aware of the gift she has made in making people, like my Mother, feel they have a real friend on their side and that their disability is not something to be ashamed of ... She has made a remarkable change to my Mother's attitude towards accepting help yet has allowed her to feel she is still independent; nothing seems too much bother for her.'

In 2004 the Community Workers made nearly 8,000 individual visits to people in their own homes.

The need to take the Association's service out to other parts of the county was forcefully made to me in 1992 when I first visited the Hunstanton Blind Club and exhorted them to visit the Equipment Centre

Charity shop in Magdalen Street, 2003

Holiday in Llandudno, 2003

in Norwich. One lady put up her hand and said words to the effect 'Boy, I have no friend with a car, I am blind, I am aged 90 and anyway Norwich is 45 miles from Hunstanton and wouldn't it be best if the Association brought its service out'. She capped the argument by saying she also needed to stop twice on each journey. The case was made!

The consequent increase in the number of Equipment & Information Centres (now also in King's Lynn, Great Yarmouth, Diss, Cromer and a Mobile Trailer) has been in response to this advice, enabling blind and partially sighted people to find suitable equipment to help them maintain their independence. Technology is moving fast and the Association has to ensure it continues to be able to show people what equipment is available to help them. This means making sure that the Association has a wide variety of equipment ranging from, for example, a liquid level indicator through to such devices as talking watches, talking microwaves and CCTVs which enlarge print and which are now being produced in a hand-held version. Fortunately manufacturers visit the Association and hold over 20 exhibitions a year throughout the County. Additionally there is a great deal of financial support from local organizations and individuals which has enabled the Association to buy some 40 large CCTVs for loan to people in their homes; many donors like to know what their donation is buying and these CCTVs are an excellent use of such money.

Sailing on Barton Broad, 2004

Just because people cannot see does not mean they cannot do anything. It is with the development of activities to stimulate the mind and body that the Association can move forward whilst still maintaining the essential work of the Community Workers, the Equipment and Information Centres, together with the excellent work of the volunteers in the Eye Clinics, as Telefriends and in the many other fields throughout the Association. The work of the 280 volunteers who support many of these activities is crucial and is the lifeblood of the Association; without them we could not do many of the things which naturally happen. The volunteers need to be cherished and respected.

The King's Lynn team, 2004

Extensive local research has been carried out and visits have been made to other Blind Charities who are facing similar challenges. As a result the Association has long recognized that it should do more to meet the ever increasing needs of many active blind and partially sighted people of all ages.

A small start has been made with computer, Braille, Moon, craft, painting and creative writing classes which are being held in Norwich but these only scratch the surface. A measure of the interest in such classes is that one 94 year old lady regularly came to Norwich on the bus from Ludham, a distance of 15 miles, to attend the computer classes.

It is important not to forget those living further afield throughout the County and Braille classes have just been started in Great Yarmouth. If this is a success further classes will start in King's Lynn. Similarly, computer classes are starting in Great Yarmouth and King's Lynn on a trial basis. The classes held in Norwich have been a tremendous success due to two excellent Adult Education Service tutors provided by the County Council. However, so far it has been very difficult to get the Adult Education Service to provide help elsewhere in the County.

Technology and mastering the skills of technology is an essential way in which people with failing sight can both stay in employment and also obtain employment. The Association is increasingly being asked for advice over employment issues and ideally should have an employment adviser; however excellent support is already given by the larger national blind charities.

The Association has also recently appointed a Sports & Leisure Co-ordinator to spread limited swimming, sailing, tandem cycling and walking activities throughout the County. It is inspiring to see what can be done. For example, two ladies aged 92 and 86 attend the sailing week-ends at Barton Broad.

Currently the Association has plans to build an Activity Centre on the site of a former workshop in Norwich which it bought back a few years ago; the building has been knocked down and the Association has raised £500,000 towards the £1.2m required.

The Activity Centre will have a large meeting room which can be sub-divided for keep-fit, dancing, lectures, etc; rooms for recording tapes and Braille; and specialist facilities to replace the inadequate ad hoc arrangements for computer, Braille, Moon and craft classes, which are already over subscribed.

A special Low Vision Aid Clinic room will be included to help cut down the long NHS waiting lists and give training in the use of low vision aids. Additional training is most important since without it people become discouraged and do not use the equipment to full potential. This is a waste of valuable NHS money. Having the service more easily

Providing help for the partially sighted, 2005

accessible to visually impaired people would enable them to benefit from improved support in the use of this equipment.

The Activity Centre will also house the present Equipment Centre bringing all the facilities that benefit visually impaired people under one roof. This will have the added advantage that people could combine taking part in activities with visits to the Equipment Centre to see what is available. It is envisaged that the existing Equipment Centre, which is adjacent to Thomas Tawell House, would then become an excellent Day Centre.

From present data it is estimated that the Activity Centre would be readily accessible to the 4,000 blind and partially sighted people within the greater Norwich area as well as a further 2,500 living within a 15–20 mile radius of Norwich. The provision of an Activity Centre would greatly help in keeping people active and stimulated and increase their confidence.

Sheringham Park, 2005

The gardens in 2005

I firmly believe that the future of the Association should be to expand its present services in close co-operation with the Sensory Support Team of Norfolk Social Services. Our services must evolve and be responsive to the needs of blind and partially sighted people. The Association really does, and continues to, make a difference to people's lives.

Safeguarding our financial resources is a key factor in these plans if we are to continue to help people. We receive generous financial support from local individuals and organizations and I think this is because we are seen around and about the County helping people.

If we stand still we will not flourish. If we look after people and listen to what they want and improve our services all the time, the legacy of Thomas Tawell will be secure.

Chairmen and Superintendents/Directors since 1890

Chairmen

1890	Canon Copeman
1896	Thomas Gillett
1898	Archdeacon Crosse
1901	Sir Charles Gilman
1908	Colonel H. T. S. Patteson
1915	Walter S. Gurney
1917	Canon Pelham
1918	Edwin B. Southwell
1922	Major, later Colonel, R. W. Patteson
1926	C. R. A. Hammond
1959	H. W. Back
1967	K. B. Riches
1976	P. Scarfe
1980	H. G. Back
1983	D. W. Trower
1984	A. Clark
1986	S. S. F. Hornor
1989	K. W. Oelrichs
1994	Mrs T. C. (Robin) Eaton
2003	Mrs Sarah Adler

Superintendents

1890	John Shave
1911	J. B. Clements
1930	R. C. Fanthorpe
1945	Alfred E. Ledger
1964	R. W. Grimsay
1982	Miss Sheila Thackeray

Directors

1989	Miss Sheila Thackeray
1992	P. J. S. (John) Child

Footnotes

The archives of the NNAB are held at the Norfolk Record Office. References to this source are not included in the footnotes. All the photographs in the book are also in the archive.

1 Phillips, Gordon *The Blind in British Society* (2004) passim
2 Phillips *op cit* p 91
3 NRO, WLS xlviii/44/9
4 NRO, DCN 26/37
5 Anon *Memoir of the late John Gurney* (no date) p 11
6 NRO, DCN 26/37
7 NRO, N/TC 35/1/3
8 Phillips, *op. cit.*
9 Rose, June *Changing Focus: the development of blind welfare in Britain* (1970)